Married Life:

Its Shadows and Sunshine

TO those who have never tried the experiment, the management of a husband may seem a very easy matter. I thought so once, but a few years' hard experience has compelled me to change my mind. When I married Mr. John Smith, which was about ten years ago, I was not altogether blind to his faults and peculiarities; but then he had so many solid virtues, that these were viewed as minor considerations. Besides, I flattered myself that it would be the easiest thing in the world to correct what was not exactly to my taste. It is no matter of especial wonder that I should have erred in this, for Mr. John Smith, while a lover, really appeared to have no will of his own, and no thought of himself. It was only necessary for me to express a wish, and it was gratified.

I soon found, much to my disappointment, that there is a marked difference between a husband and a lover: it was at least so in the case of Mr. Smith, and observation, since I have had my eyes open, satisfies me that it is so in most cases. I must own, in justice to all parties, however, that this difference is made more apparent by a want of knowledge, on the other side, in regard to the difference between the relation of a wife and a sweetheart—between the wooed and the won.

There were a good many little things in Mr. Smith, which I had noticed before marriage, that I made up my mind to correct as soon as I had an opportunity to apply the proper means. He had a fashion of saying "Miss" for "Mrs.," as "Miss Jones" and "Miss Peters" for "Mrs. Jones" and "Mrs. Peters." This sounded exceedingly vulgar to my ears, and I waited almost impatiently for the time to come when I could use the prerogative of a wife for its correction. He had, an ungraceful way of lounging in his chair and half reclining on the sofa, even in company, that was terrible. It made me uneasy from head to foot. Then he said, "I *shew* it to him" for "I *showed* it to him,"—"of-*ten*" for "oft'n"—and "*obleeged*" for "obliged."

Besides these, there were sundry other things that worried me not a little. But I consoled myself with the reflection that when I became Mrs. Smith all these little matters would vanish like frost in the sunshine. I was, alas! doomed to be mistaken. But let me give my experience for the benefit of those who are to come after me.

We had been married just ten days, and I had begun to feel that I was really a wife, and had a right to say and do a little as I pleased, when Mr. Smith said to me, as we sat quite lover-like on the sofa in the evening,

"I met Miss Williams as I came home this evening—"

"For mercy's sake, Mr. Smith! don't say *Miss* when you speak of a married woman. It is excessively vulgar." I was not aware that I had spoken in a very offensive way, but I noticed an instant change in Mr. Smith. He replied, with some dignity of tone, and manner—

"I ask your pardon, madam; but I didn't say *Miss*. I am not quite so ignorant as all that comes to."

"Oh, yes, Mr. Smith, but you did say it," I replied, quite astonished at this unexpected denial.

"Excuse me for saying that you are in error," he returned, drawing himself up. "I never say Miss for Mrs."

"Why, Mr. Smith! You always say it. I have noticed it a hundred times. I believe I can hear pretty correctly."

"In this instance you certainly have not."

Mr. Smith was growing warm, and I felt the blood rushing to my face. A rather tart reply was on my lips, but I bit them hard and succeeded in keeping them closed.

A deep silence followed. In a little while Mr. Smith took up a newspaper and commenced reading, and I found some relief for a heavy pressure that was upon my bosom, in the employment of hem-stitching a fine pocket-handkerchief.

And this was the return I had met for a kind attempt to correct a mistake of my husband's, that made him liable to ridicule on the charge of vulgarity! And to deny, too, that he said "*Miss*," when I had been worried about it for more than a year! It was too bad!

After this Mr. Smith was very particular in saying, when he spoke of a married woman to me, *Misses*. The emphasis on the second syllable was much too strongly marked to be pleasant on my ears. I was terribly afraid he would say "*Mistress*," thus going off into the opposite extreme of vulgarity.

This first attempt to put my husband straight had certainly not been a very pleasant one. He had shown, unexpectedly to me, a humour that could by no means be called amiable; and by which I was both grieved, and astonished. I made up my mind that I would be very careful in future how I tried my hand at reforming him. But his oft-repeated "he *shew* it to me," and "*obleeged.*," soon fretted me so sorely, that I was forced to come down upon him again, which I did at a time when I felt more than usually annoyed. I cannot remember now precisely what I said to him, but I know that I put him into an ill-humour, and that it was cloudy weather in the house for a week, although the sun shone brightly enough out of doors. "*He shew it to me.*," and "*obleeged*" were, however, among the things that had been, after that. So much was gained; although there were times when I half suspected that I had lost more than I had gained. But I persevered, and, every now and then, when I got "worked up" about something, administered the rod of correction.

Gradually I could see that my husband was changing, and, as I felt, for the worse. Scarcely a year had passed before he would get into a pet if I said the least word to him. He couldn't bear any thing from me. This seemed very unreasonable, and caused me not only to sigh, but to shed many a tear over his perverseness. From the thoughtful, ever considerate, self-sacrificing lover, he had come to be disregardful of my wishes, careless of my comfort, and indifferent to my society. Still I felt by no means inclined to give him up; was by no means disposed to let him have his own way. It was clear to my mind that I had rights as well as he had; and I possessed resolution enough to be ready to maintain them. His self-will and indifference to my wishes roused in me a bitter and contentious spirit; and, in an evil hour, I determined that I would make a struggle for the mastery. An opportunity was not long delayed. The Philharmonic Society had announced one of its splendid concerts. A lady friend, who had frequently attended these concerts, called in to see me, and, by what she said, filled me with a desire to enjoy the fine musical treat that had been announced for that very evening.

When Mr. Smith came home at dinner he said, before I had time to mention the concert—

"Mary, I've taken a fancy to go and see Fanny Ellsler to-night, and, as there will be no chance of getting a good seat this afternoon, I took the precaution to secure tickets as I came home to dinner. I would have sent the porter with a note to know whether there was any thing to prevent your going to-night, but he has been out all the morning, and I concluded that, even if there should be some slight impediment in the way, you could easily set it aside."

Now this I thought too much. To go and buy tickets to see Fanny Ellsler dance, and take it for granted that I would lay every thing aside to go, when I had set my heart on attending the Philharmonic concert!

"You are a strange man, Mr. Smith," said I. "You ought to know that I don't care a fig about seeing Fanny Ellsler. I don't relish such kind of performances. You at least might have waited until you came home to dinner and asked the question. I don't believe a word about the good seats all being taken this morning. But it's just like you! To go and see this dancers toss her feet about was a thing you had made up your mind to do, and I was to go along whether I liked it or not."

"You talk in rather a strange way, Mrs. Smith," said my husband, evidently offended.

"I don't see that I do," replied I, warming. "The fact is, Mr. Smith, you seem to take it for granted that I am nobody. Here I've been making all my calculations to go to the Philharmonic to-night, and you come home with tickets for the theatre! But I can tell you plainly that I am *not* going to see Fanny Ellsler, and that I *am* going to the Philharmonic."

This was taking a stand that I had never taken before. In most of my efforts to make my husband go my way, he had succeeded in making me go his way. This always chafed me dreadfully. I fretted and scolded, and "all that sort of thing," but it was no use, I could not manage him. The direct issue of "I won't" and "I will" had not yet been made, and I was some time in coming to the resolution to have a struggle, fiercer than ever, for the ascendency. I fondly believed that for peace' sake he would not stand firm if he saw me resolute. Under this view of the case, I made the open averment that I would not go to the theatre. I expected that a scene would follow, but I was mistaken. Mr. Smith did, indeed, open his eyes a little wider, but he said nothing.

Just then the bell announced that dinner was on the table. Mr. Smith arose and led the way to the dinner-room with a firm step. Before we were married he wouldn't have dreamed of thus preceding me! I was fretted at this little act. It indicated too plainly what was in the man.

Dinner passed in silence. I forced myself to eat, that I might appear unconcerned. On rising from the table, Mr. Smith left the house without saying a word.

You may suppose I didn't feel very comfortable during the afternoon. I had taken my stand, and my intention was to maintain it to the last. That Mr. Smith would yield I had no doubt at first. But, as evening approached, and the trial-time drew near, I had some misgivings.

Mr. Smith came home early.

"Mary," said he, in his usual pleasant way, "I have ordered a carriage to be here at half-past seven. We mustn't leave home later, as the curtain rises at eight."

"What curtain rises? Where do you think of going?"

"To see Fanny Ellsler, of course. I mentioned to you at dinner-time that I had tickets."

This was said very calmly.

"And I told you at dinner-time that I was going to the Philharmonic, and not to see this dancer." I tried to appear as composed as he was, but failed in the attempt altogether.

"You were aware that I had tickets for the theatre before you said that," was the cold answer he made.

"Of course I was."

"Very well, Mary. You can do as you like. The carriage will be here at half-past seven. If you are then ready to go to the theatre, I shall be happy to have your company." And my husband, after saying this with a most unruffled manner, politely bowed and retired to the parlour.

I was on fire. But I had no thought of yielding.

At half-past seven I was ready. I heard the carriage drive up to the door and the bell ring.

"Mary," called my husband at the bottom of the stair-case, in a cheerful tone, "are you ready?"

"Ready to go where?" I asked on descending.

"To the theatre."

"I am ready for the concert," I answered in as composed a voice as I could assume.

"*I* am not going to the concert to-night, Mrs. Smith. I thought you understood that," firmly replied my husband. "I am going to see Fanny Ellsler. If you will go with me, I shall be very happy to have your company. If not, I must go alone."

"And I am going to the Philharmonic. I thought you understood that," I replied, with equal resolution.

"Oh! very well," said he, not seeming to be at all disturbed. "Then you can use the carriage at the door. I will walk to the theatre."

Saying this, Mr. Smith turned from me deliberately and walked away. I heard him tell the driver of the carriage to take me to the Musical Fund Hall; then I heard the street-door close, and then I heard my husband's footsteps on the pavement as he left the house. Without hesitating a moment for reflection, I followed to the door, entered the carriage, and ordered the man to drive me—where? I had no ticket for the concert; nor could I go alone!

"To the Musical Fund Hall, I believe, madam," he said, standing with his fingers touching the rim of his hat.

I tried to think what I should do. To be conquered was hard. And it was clear that I could not go alone.

"No," I replied, grasping hold of the first suggestion that came to my mind. "Drive me to No.—Walnut street."

I had directed him to the house of my sister, where I thought I would stay until after eleven o'clock, and then return home, leaving my husband to infer that I had been to the concert. But long before I had reached my sister's house, I felt so miserable that I deemed it best to call out of the window to the driver, and direct him to return. On arriving at home, some twenty minutes after I had left it, I went up to my chamber, and there had a hearty crying spell to myself. I don't know that I ever felt so bad before in my life. I had utterly failed in this vigorous contest with my husband, who had come off perfectly victorious. Many bitter things did I write against him in my heart, and largely did I magnify his faults. I believe I thought over every thing that occurred since we were married, and selected therefrom whatever could justify the conclusion that he was a self-willed, overbearing, unfeeling man, and did not entertain for me a particle of affection.

It was clear that I had not been able to manage my spouse, determined as I had been to correct all his faults, and make him one of the best, most conciliating and loving of husbands, with whom my wish would be law. Still I could not think of giving up. The thought of being reduced to a tame, submissive wife, who could hardly call her soul her own, was not for a moment to be entertained. On reflection, it occurred to me that I had, probably, taken the wrong method with my husband. There was a touch of stubbornness in his nature that had arrayed itself against my too earnest efforts to bend him to my will. A better way occurred. I had heard it said by some one, or had read it somewhere, that no man was proof against a woman's tears.

On the present occasion I certainly felt much more like crying than laughing, and so it was no hard matter, I can honestly aver, to appear bathed in tears on my husband's return between eleven and twelve o'clock from the theatre. I cried from vexation as much as from any other feeling.

When Mr. Smith came up into the chamber where I lay, I greeted his presence with half a dozen running sobs, which he answered by whistling the "Craccovienne!" I continued to sob, and he continued to whistle for the next ten minutes. By that time he was ready to get into bed, which he did quite leisurely, and laid himself down upon his pillow with an expression of satisfaction. Still I sobbed on, thinking that every sighing breath I drew was, in spite of his seeming indifference, a pang to his heart. But, from this fond delusion a heavily drawn breath, that was almost a snore, aroused me. I raised up and looked over at the man—he was sound asleep.

A good hearty cry to myself was all the satisfaction I had, and then I went to sleep. On the next morning, I met Mr. Smith at the breakfast table with red eyes and a sad countenance. But he did not seem to notice either.

"I hope you enjoyed yourself at the concert last night," said he. "I was delighted at the theatre. Fanny danced divinely. Hers is truly the poetry of motion!"

Now this was too much! I will leave it to any reader—any female reader, I mean—whether this was not too much. I burst into a flood of tears and immediately withdrew, leaving my husband to eat his breakfast alone. He sat the usual time, which provoked me exceedingly. If he had jumped up from the table and left the house, I would have felt that I had made some impression upon him. But to take things in this calm way! What had I gained? Nothing, as I could see. After breakfast Mr. Smith came up to the chamber, and, seeing my face buried in a pillow, weeping bitterly—I had increased the flow of tears on hearing him ascending the stairs—said in a low voice—

"Are you not well, Mary?"

I made no answer, but continued to weep. Mr. Smith stood for the space of about a minute, but asked no further question. Then, without uttering a word, he retired from the chamber, and in a little while after I heard him leave the house. I cried now in good earnest. It was plain that my husband had no feeling; that he did not care whether I was pleased or sad. But I determined to give him a fair trial. If I failed in this new way, what was I to do? The thought of becoming the passive slave of a domestic tyrant was dreadful. I felt that I could not live in such a state. When Mr. Smith came home at dinner-time I was in my chamber, ready prepared for a gush of tears. As he opened the door I looked up with streaming eyes, and then hid my face in a pillow.

"Mary," said he, with much kindness in his voice, "what ails you? Are you sick?" He laid his hand upon mine as he spoke.

But I did not reply. I meant to punish him well for what he had done as a lesson for the future. I next expected him to draw his arm around me, and be very tender and sympathizing in his words and tones. But no such thing! He quietly withdrew the hand he had placed upon mine; and stood by me, I could feel, though not see, in a cold, erect attitude.

"Are you not well, Mary?" he asked again.

I was still silent. A little while after I heard him moving across the floor, and then the chamber door shut. I was once more alone.

When the bell rang for dinner, I felt half sorry that I had commenced this new mode of managing my husband; but, as I had begun, I was determined to go through with it. "He'll at least take care how he acts in the future," I said. I did not leave my chamber to join my husband at the dinner table. He sat his usual time, as I could tell by the ringing of the bell for the servant to change the plates and bring in the dessert. I was exceedingly fretted; and more so by his returning to his business without calling up to see me, and making another effort to dispel my grief.

For three days I tried this experiment upon my husband, who bore it with the unflinching heroism of a martyr. I was forced, at last, to come to; but I was by no means satisfied that my new mode was a failure. For all Mr. Smith's assumed indifference, I knew that he had been troubled at heart, and I was pretty well satisfied that he would think twice before provoking me to another essay of tears. Upon the whole, I felt pretty sure that I had discovered the means of doing with him as I pleased.

A few weeks of sunshine passed—I must own that the sun did not look so bright, nor feel so warm as it had done in former times—and then our wills came once more into collision. But my tears fell upon a rock. I could not see that they made the least perceptible impression. Mr. Smith had his own way, and I cried about it until I got tired of that sport, and in very weariness gave over. For the space of a whole year I stood upon tears as my last defensible position. Sometimes I didn't smile for weeks. But my husband maintained his ground like a hero.

At last I gave up in despair. Pride, self-will, anger—all were conquered. I was a weak woman in the hands of a strong-minded man. If I could not love him as I wished to love him, I could at least obey. In nothing did I now oppose him, either by resolute words or tears. If he expressed a wish, whether to me agreeable or not, I acquiesced.

One day, not long after this change in my conduct towards my husband, he said to me, "I rather think, Mary, we will spend a couple of weeks at Brandywine Springs, instead of going to Cape May this season."

I replied, "Very well, dear;" although I had set my heart on going to the Capes. My sister and her husband and a number of my friends were going down, and I had anticipated a good deal of pleasure. I did not know of a single person who was going to the Brandywine Springs. But what was the use of entering into a contest with my husband? He would come off the conqueror, spite of angry words or ineffectual tears.

"The Springs are so much more quiet than the Capes," said my husband.

"Yes," I remarked, "there is less gay company there."

"Don't you think you will enjoy yourself as well there as at the Capes?"

Now this was a good deal for my husband to say. I hardly knew what to make of it.

"If you prefer going there, dear, let us go by all means," I answered. I was not affecting any thing, but was in earnest in what I said.

Mr. Smith looked into my face for some moments, and with unusual affection I thought.

"Mary," said he, "if you think the time will pass more pleasantly to you at the Capes, let us go there by all means."

"My sister Jane is going to the Capes," I remarked, with some little hesitation; "and so is Mrs. L—and Mrs. D—, and a good many more of our friends. I did think that I would enjoy myself there this season very much. But I have no doubt I shall find pleasant society at the Springs."

"We will go to the Capes," said my husband promptly and cheerfully.

"No," said I, emulous now for the first time in a new cause. "I am sure the time will pass agreeably enough at the Springs. And as you evidently prefer going there, we will let the Capes pass for this year."

"To the Capes, Mary, and nowhere else," replied my husband, in the very best of humours. "I am sure you will enjoy yourself far better there. I did not know your sister was going."

And to the Capes we went, and I did enjoy myself excellently well. As for my husband, I never saw him in a better state of mind. To me he was more like a lover than a husband. No, I will not say that either, for I can't admit that a husband may not be as kind and affectionate as a lover; for he can and will be if managed rightly, and a great deal more so. Whenever I expressed a wish, it appeared to give him pleasure to gratify it. Seeing this, instead of suffering myself to be the mere recipient of kind attentions, I began to vie with him in the sacrifice of selfish wishes and feelings.

It is wonderful how all was changed after this. There were no more struggles on my part to manage my husband, and yet I generally had things my own way. Before I could not turn him to the right nor the left, though I strove to do so with my utmost strength. Now I held him only with a silken fetter, and guided him, without really intending to do so, in almost any direction.

Several years have passed since that ever-to-be-remembered, happy visit to Cape May. Not once since have I attempted any management of my husband, and yet it is a rare thing that my wish is not, as it used to be before we were married, his law. It is wonderful, too, how he has improved. I am sure he is not the same man that he was five years ago. But, perhaps, I see with different eyes. At any rate, I am not the same woman; or, if the same, very unlike what I then was.

So much for my efforts to manage a husband. Of the three ways so faithfully tried, my fair readers will be at no loss to determine which is best. I make these honest confessions for the good of my sex. My husband, Mr. John Smith, will be no little surprised if this history should meet his eye. But I do not believe it will interrupt the present harmonious relations existing between us, but rather tend to confirm and strengthen them.

RULING A WIFE.

AS a lover, Henry Lane was the kindest, most devoted, self-sacrificing person imaginable. He appeared really to have no will of his own, so entire was his deference to his beautiful Amanda; yet, for all this, he had no very high opinion of her as an intelligent being. She was lovely, she was gentle, she was good; and these qualities, combined with personal grace and beauty, drew him in admiration to her side, and filled him with the desire to possess her as his own.

As a husband, Henry Lane was a different being. His relation had changed, and his exterior changed correspondingly. Amanda was his wife; and as such she must be, in a certain sense, under him. It was his judgment that must govern in all matters; for her judgment, in the affairs of life, was held in light estimation. Moreover, as a man, it was his province to control and direct and her duty to look to him for guidance.

Yet, for all this, if the truth must be told, the conclusions of Amanda's mind were, in ordinary affairs, even more correct than her husband's judgment; for he was governed a great deal by impulses and first impressions, instead of by the reason of which he was so proud, while she came naturally into the woman's quick perceptions of right and propriety. This being the case, it may readily be seen that there was a broad groundwork for unhappiness in the married state. Amanda could not sink into a mere cipher; she could not give up her will entirely to the guidance of another, and cease to act from her own volitions.

It took only a few months to make the young wife feel that her position was to be one of great trial. She was of a mild and gentle character, more inclined to suffer than resist; but her judgment was clear, and she saw the right or wrong of any act almost instinctively. Love did not make her blind to every thing in her husband. He had faults and unpleasant peculiarities, and she saw them plainly, and often desired to correct them. But one trial of this kind sufficed to keep her silent. He was offended, and showed his state of mind so plainly, that she resolved never to stand in that relation to him again.

As time progressed, the passiveness of Amanda encouraged in Lane his natural love of ruling. His household was his kingdom, and there his will must be the law. In his mind arose the conceit that, in every thing, his judgment was superior to that of his wife: even in the smaller matters of household economy, he let this be seen. His taste, too, was more correct, and applied itself to guiding and directing her into a proper state of dressing. He decided about the harmony of colours and the choice of patterns. She could not buy even a ribbon without there being some fault found with it, as not possessing the elements of beauty in just arrangements. In company, you would often hear him say—"Oh, my wife has no taste. She would dress like a fright if I did not watch her all the time."

Though outwardly passive or concurrent when such things were said, Amanda felt them as unjust, and they wounded her more or less severely, according to the character of the company in which she happened at the time to be; but her self-satisfied husband saw nothing of this. And not even when some one, more plainly spoken than others, would reply to such a remark—"She did not dress like a fright before you were married," did he perceive his presumption and his errors.

But passiveness under such a relation does not always permanently remain; it was accompanied from the first by a sense of oppression and injustice, though love kept the feeling subdued. The desire for ruling in any position gains strength by activity. The more the young wife yielded, the more did the husband assume, until at length Amanda felt that she had no will of her own, so to speak. The conviction of this, when it formed itself in her mind, half involuntarily brought with it an instinctive feeling of resistance. Here was the forming point of antagonism—the beginning of the state of unhappiness foreshadowed from the first. Had Amanda asserted her right to think and act for herself in the early days of her married life, the jar of discord would have been light. It now promised to be most afflicting in its character.

The first activity of Amanda's newly forming state showed itself in the doing of certain things to which she was inclined, notwithstanding the expression of her husband's disapproval. Accustomed to the most perfect compliance, Mr. Lane was disturbed by this.

"Oh, dear! what a horrid looking thing!" said he one day, as he discovered a new dress pattern which his wife had just purchased lying on a chair. "Where in the world did that come from?"

"I bought it this morning," replied Amanda.

"Take it back, or throw it into the fire," was the husband's rude response.

"I think it neat," said Amanda, smiling.

"Neat? It's awful! But you've no taste. I wish you'd let me buy your dresses."

The wife made no answer to this. Lane said a good deal more about it, to all of which Amanda opposed but little. However, her mind was made up to one thing, and that was to take it to the mantuamaker's. The next Lane saw of the dress was on his wife.

"Oh, mercy!" he exclaimed, holding up his hand, "I thought you had burnt it. Why did you have it made up?"

"I like it," quietly answered Mrs. Lane.

"You like any thing."

"I haven't much taste, I know," said Amanda, "but such as it is, it is pleasant to gratify it sometimes."

Something in the way this remark was made it disturbed the self-satisfaction which was a leading feature in Mr. Lane's state of mind; he, however, answered—"I wish you would be governed by me in matters of this kind; you know my taste is superior to yours. Do take off that dress, and throw it in the fire."

Amanda did not reply to this, for it excited feelings and produced thoughts that she had no wish to manifest. But she did not comply with her husband's wishes. She liked the dress and meant to wear it, and she did wear it, notwithstanding her husband's repeated condemnation of her taste.

At this time they had one child—a babe less than a year old. From the first, Lane had encroached upon the mother's province. This had been felt more sensibly than any thing else by his wife, for it disturbed the harmonious activity of the natural law which gives to a mother the perception of what is best for her infant. Still, she had been so in the habit of yielding to the force of his will, that she gave way to his interference here in numberless instances, though she as often felt that he was wrong as right. Conceit of his own intelligence blinded him to the intelligence of others. Of this Amanda became more and more satisfied every day. At first, she had passively admitted that he knew best; but her own common sense and clear perceptions soon repudiated this idea. While his love of predominance affected only herself, she could bear it with great patience; but when it was exercised, day after day, and week after week, in matters pertaining to her babe, she grew restless under the oppression.

After the decided, position taken in regard to her dress, Amanda's mind acquired strength in a new direction. A single gratification of her own will, attained in opposition to the will of her husband, stirred a latent desire for repeated gratifications; and it was not long before Lane discovered this fact, and wondered at the change which had taken place in his wife's temper. She no longer acquiesced in every suggestion, nor yielded when he opposed argument to an assumed position. The pleasure of thinking and acting for herself had been restored, and the delight appertaining to its indulgence was no more to be suppressed. Her husband's reaction on this state put her in greater freedom; for it made more distinctly manifest the quality of his ruling affection, and awoke in her mind a more determined spirit of resistance.

Up to this time, even in the most trifling matters of domestic and social life, Lane's will had been the law. This was to be so no longer. A new will had come into activity; and that will a woman's will. Passive it had been for a long time under a pressure that partial love and a yielding temper permitted to remain; but its inward life was unimpaired; and when its motions became earnest, it was strong and enduring. The effort made by Lane to subdue these motions the moment he perceived them, only gave them a stronger impulse. The hand laid upon her heart to quiet its pulsations only made it beat with a quicker effort, while it communicated its disturbance to his own.

The causes leading to the result we are to describe have been fully enough set forth; they steadily progressed until the husband and wife were in positions of direct antagonism. Lane could not give up his love of controlling every thing around him, and his wife, fairly roused to opposition, followed the promptings of her own will, in matters where right was clearly on her side, with a quiet perseverance that always succeeded. Of course, they were often made unhappy; yet enough forbearance existed on both sides to prevent an open rupture—at least, for a time. That, however, came at last, and was the more violent from the long accumulation of reactive forces.

The particulars of this rupture we need not give; it arose in a dispute about the child when she was two years old. As usual, Lane had attempted to set aside the judgment of his wife in something pertaining to the child, as inferior to his own, and she had not submitted. Warm words ensued, in which he said a good deal about a wife's knowing her place and keeping it.

"I am not your slave!" said Amanda, indignantly; the cutting words of her husband throwing her off her guard.

"You are my wife," he calmly and half contemptuously replied; "and, as such, are bound to submit yourself to your husband."

"To my husband's intelligence, not to his mere will," answered Amanda, less warmly, but more resolutely than at first.

"Yes, to his will!" said Lane, growing blind from anger.

"That I have done long enough," returned the wife. "But the time is past now. By your intelligence, when I see in it superior light to what exists in my own, I will be guided, but, by your will—never!"

The onward moving current of years, which, for some time, had been chafing amid obstructions, now met a sudden barrier, and flowed over in a raging torrent. A sharp retort met this firm declaration of Amanda, stinging her into anger, and producing a state of recrimination. While in this state, she spoke plainly of his assumption of authority over her from the first,—of her passiveness for a time,—of being finally aroused to opposition.

"And now," she added, in conclusion, "I am content to be your wife and equal, but will be no longer your passive and obedient slave."

"Your duty is to obey. You can occupy no other position as my wife," returned the blind and excited husband.

"Then we must part."

"Be it so." And as he said this, Lane turned hurriedly away and left the house.

Fixed as a statue, for a long time, sat the stunned and wretched wife. As the current of thoughts again flowed on, and the words of her husband presented themselves in even a more offensive light than when they were first uttered, indignant pride took the uppermost place in her mind.

"He will not treat me as a wife and equal," she said, "and I will no longer be his slave."

In anger Lane turned from his wife; and for hours after parting with her this anger burned with an all-consuming flame. For him to yield was out of the question. His manly pride would never consent to this. She must fall back into her true position. He did not return home, as usual, at dinner-time; but absented himself, in order to give her time for reflection, as well as to awaken her fears lest he would abandon her altogether. Towards night, imagining his wife in a state of penitence and distressing anxiety, and feeling some commiseration for her on that account, Mr. Lane went back to his dwelling. As he stepped within the door, a feeling of desertion and loneliness came over him; and unusual silence seemed to pervade the house. He sat down in the parlour for some minutes; but hearing no movement in the chamber above, nor catching even a murmur of his child's voice, a sound for which his ears were longing, he ascended the stairs, but found no one there. As he turned to go down again he met a servant.

"Where is Mrs. Lane?" he asked.

"I don't know," was answered. "She went out this morning, and has not returned."

"Where is Mary?"

"She took Mary with her."

"Didn't she say where she was going?"

"No, sir."

Mr. Lane asked no more questions, but went back into the room from which he had just emerged, and, sitting down, covered his face with his hands, and endeavoured to collect his thoughts.

"Has she deserted me?" he asked of himself in an audible husky whisper.

His heart grew faint in the pause that followed. As the idea of desertion became more and more distinct, Mr. Lane commenced searching about in order to see whether his wife had not left some communication for him, in which her purpose was declared. But he found none. She had departed without leaving a sign. The night that followed was a sleepless one to Lane. His mind was agitated by many conflicting emotions. For hours, on the next day, he remained at home, in the expectation of seeing or hearing from

Amanda. But no word came. Where had she gone? That was the next question. If he must go in search of hers in what direction should he turn his steps? She had no relations in the city, and with those who resided at a distance she had cultivated no intimacy.

The whole day was passed in a state of irresolution. To make the fact known was to expose a family difficulty that concerned only himself and wife; and give room for idle gossip and gross detraction. Bad as the case was, the public would make it appear a great deal worse than the reality. In the hope of avoiding this, he concealed the sad affair for the entire day, looking, in each recurring hour, for the return of his repentant wife. But he looked in vain. Night came gloomily down, and she was still absent.

He was sitting, about eight o'clock in the evening, undetermined yet what to do, when a gentleman with whom he was but slightly acquainted named Edmondson, called at the door and asked to see him.

On being shown in, the latter, with some embarrassment in his manner, said—

"I have called to inform you, that Mrs. Lane has been at my house since yesterday."

"At *your* house!"

"Yes. She came there yesterday morning; and, since that time, my wife has been doing her best to induce her to return home. But, so far, she has not been able to make the smallest impression. Not wishing to become a party to the matter, I have called to see you on the subject. I regret, exceedingly, that any misunderstanding has occurred, and do not intend that either myself or family shall take sides in so painful an affair. All that I can do, however, to heal the difficulty, shall be done cheerfully."

"What does she say?" asked Lane, when he had composed himself.

"She makes no specific complaint."

"What does she propose doing?"

"She avows her intention of living separate from you, and supporting herself and child by her own efforts."

This declaration aroused a feeling of indignant pride in the husband's mind. "It is my child as well as hers," said he. "She may desert me, if she will; but she cannot expect me to give up my child. To that I will never submit."

"My dear sir," said Mr. Edmondson, "do not permit your mind to chafe, angrily, over this unhappy matter. That will widen not heal, the breach. In affairs of this kind, pardon me for the remark, there are always faults on both sides; and the duty of each is to put away his or her own state of anger and antagonism and seek to reconcile the other, rather than to compel submission. As a man, you have the advantage of a stronger and clearer judgment,—exercise it as a man. Feeling and impulse often rule in a woman's mind, from the very nature of her mental conformation; and we should remember this when we pass judgment on her actions. There is often more honour in yielding a point than in contending for it to the end, in the face of threatened disaster. Let me then urge you to seek a reconciliation, while there is yet opportunity, and permit the veil of oblivion to fall, while it may, over this painful event. As yet, the fact has not passed from the knowledge of myself and wife. Heal the breach, and the secret remains where it is."

"If she will return, I will receive her, and forgive and forget all. Will you say this to her from me?"

"Why not go to her at once? See her face to face. This is the best and surest way."

"No," said Lane, coldly. "She has left me of her own choice; and, now, she must return. I gave her no cause for the rash act. Enough for me that I am willing to forgive and forget all this. But I am not the man to humble myself at the feet of a capricious woman. It is not in me."

"Mr. Lane, you are wrong!" said the visitor, in a decided tone. "All wrong. Do you believe that your wife would have fled from you without a real or imagined cause?"

"No. But the cause is only in her imagination."

"Then see her and convince her of this. It is the same to her, at present, whether the cause be real or imaginary. She believes it real, and feels all its effects as real. Show her that it is imaginary, and all is healed."

Lane shook his head.

"I have never humbled myself before a man, much less a woman," said he.

This remark exhibited to Mr. Edmondson the whole ground-work of the difficulty. Lane regarded a woman as inferior to a man, and had for her, in consequence, a latent feeling of contempt. He could understand, now, why his wife had left him; for he saw, clearly, that, with such an estimation of woman, he would attempt to degrade her from her true position; and, if she possessed an independent spirit, render her life wellnigh insupportable. Earnestly did he seek to convince Lane of his error; but to no good effect. As soon as all doubt was removed from the mind of the latter in regard to where his wife had gone, and touching the spirit which governed her in her separation from him, his natural pride and self-esteem—self-respect, he called it—came back into full activity. No, he would never humble himself to a woman! That was the unalterable state of his mind. If Amanda would return, and assume her old place and her old relation, he would forget and forgive all. This far he would go, and no farther. She had left of her own free will, and that must bring her back.

"You can say all this to her in any way you please; but I will not seek her and enter into an humble supplication for her return. I have too much self-respect—and am too much of a man—for that. If she finds the struggle to do so hard and humiliating, she will be the more careful how she places herself again in such a position. The lesson will last her a life-time."

"You are wrong; depend upon it, you are wrong!" urged Mr. Edmondson. "There must be yielding and conciliation on both sides."

"I can do no more than I have said. Passive I have been from the first, and passive I will remain. As for our child, I wish you to say to her, that I shall not consent to a separation. It is my child as much as hers; moreover, as father, my responsibility is greatest, and I am not the man to delegate my duties to another. Possession of the child, if driven to that extremity, I will obtain through aid of the law. This I desire that she shall distinctly understand. I make no threat. I do not wish her to view the declaration in that light. I affirm only the truth, that she may clearly understand all the consequences likely to flow from her ill-advised step."

The more Mr. Edmondson sought to convince Mr. Lane of his error, the more determinedly did he cling to it; and he retired at last, under the sad conviction that the unhappy couple had seen but the beginning of troubles.

Alone with his own thoughts, an hour had not elapsed before Mr. Lane half repented of his conduct in taking so unyielding a position. A conviction forced itself upon his mind that he had gone too far and was asking too much; and he wished that he had not been quite so exacting in his declarations to Mr. Edmondson. But, having made them, his false pride of consistency prompted him to adhere to what he had said.

The night passed in broken and troubled sleep; and morning found him supremely wretched. Yet resentment still formed a part of Mr. Lane's feelings. He was angry with his wife, whom he had driven from his side, and was in no mood to bend in order to effect a reconciliation. At mid-day he returned from his business, hoping to find her at home. But his house was still desolate. With the evening he confidently expected her, but she was not there. Anxiously he sat, hour after hour, looking for another visit from Mr. Edmondson, but he came not again.

In leaving her husband's house, Mrs. Lane had gone, as has been seen, to the house of a friend. Mrs. Edmondson was an old school companion, between whom and herself had continued to exist, as they grew up, the tenderest relations. When she turned from her husband, she fled, with an instinct of affection and sympathy, to this friend, and poured her tears in a gild agony of affliction upon her bosom. In leaving her husband, she was not governed by a sudden caprice; nor was the act intended to humble him to her feet. Nothing of this was in her mind. He had trenched upon her province as a wife and mother; interfered with her freedom as an individual; and, at last, boldly assumed the right to command and control her as an inferior. The native independence of her character, which had long fretted under this rule of subordination, now openly rebelled, and, panting for freedom, she had sprung from her fetters with few thoughts as to future consequences.

The first day of absence was a day of weeping. Mrs. Edmondson could not and did not approve of what had been done.

"I am afraid, Amanda, that you have only made matters worse," said she, as soon as she could venture to suggest any thing at all upon the subject. "It is always easier to prevent than to heal a breach. The day has not yet closed. There is time to go back. Your husband need never know what has been in your mind. This hasty act may be entirely concealed from him."

But the long suffering wife had been roused to opposition. A new current of feeling was sweeping across and controlling her mind. She was, therefore, deaf to the voice of reason. Still her friend, as in duty bound, urged her to think more calmly on the subject, and to retrace the steps she had taken. But all was in vain. This being so, her husband, as has been seen, called upon Mr. Lane, and informed him that his wife was at his house. From this interview Mr. Edmondson returned disheartened, and reported all that had been said on both sides to his wife.

"My husband saw Mr. Lane last evening," said Mrs. Edmondson to Amanda on the next day.

"He did!" Amanda looked eagerly into the face of her friend, while she became much agitated.

"Yes. He called to let him know that you were here."

"What did he say?"

"He wishes you to return. All will be forgotten and forgiven."

"He said that?"

"Yes."

"I have done nothing for which I desire forgiveness," said Amanda, coldly, and with the air of one who is hurt by the words of another. "If he will not have me return as his wife and equal, I can never go back."

"For the sake of your child, Amanda, you should be willing to bear much."

"My child shall not grow, up and see her mother degraded."

"She is his child as well as yours. Do not forget that," said Mrs. Edmondson. "And it is by no means certain that he will permit you to retain the possession of an object so dear to him."

The face of Mrs. Lane instantly flushed at this, a suggestion which had not before been presented to her mind.

"Did he refer to this subject in conversing with your husband?" inquired Amanda, with forced calmness.

"He did."

"What did he say?"

"That, in any event, he could not and would not be separated from his child. And you know, Amanda, that the law will give to him its guardianship."

"The law!" There was a huskiness in Mrs. Lane's voice.

"Yes, Amanda, the law. It is well for you to view this matter in all its relations. The law regards the father as the true guardian of the child. If, therefore, you separate yourself from your husband, you must expect to bear a separation from your child; for that will be most likely to follow."

"Did he speak of the law?" asked Mrs. Lane, in a still calmer voice, and with a steady eye.

"It would not be right to conceal from you this fact, Amanda. He did do so. And can you wholly blame him? It is his child as well as yours. He loves it, as you well know; and, as its father, he is responsible for it to society and to Heaven. This separation is your act. You may deprive him of your own society; but, have you a right, at the same time, to rob him of his child? I speak plainly; I would not be your friend did I not do so. Try, for a little while, to look away from yourself, and think of your husband; and especially of the consequences likely to arise to your child from your present act. It will not be a mere separation with passive endurance of pain on either side. There will come the prolonged effort of the father to recover his child, and the anguish and fear of the mother, as she lives in the constant dread of having it snatched from her hands. And that must come, inevitably, the final separation. You will have to part from your child, Amanda, if not in the beginning, yet finally. You know your husband to be of a resolute temper Do not give him a chance to press you to extremity. If he should come to the determination to recover his child from your hands, he will not stop short of any means to accomplish his purpose."

Mrs. Lane made no reply to this; nor did she answer to any further remark, appeal, or suggestion of her friend, who soon ceased to speak on the subject and left her to her own reflections, hoping that they might lead her to some better purpose than had yet influenced her in the unhappy business. On the day after, Mr. Edmondson met Lane in the street.

"I was about calling to see you," said the latter, "on the subject of this unhappy difficulty, to which, so reluctantly to yourself, you have become a party. It may be that I am something to blame. Perhaps I have been too exacting—too jealous of my prerogative as a husband. At any rate, I am willing to admit that such has been the case; and willing to yield something to the morbid feelings of my wife. What is her present state of mind?"

Mr. Edmondson looked surprised.

Remarking this, Lane said quickly, "Is she not at your house?"

"No," replied Mr. Edmondson, "she left us yesterday. We believed that she had gone home. My wife had a long conversation with her, in which she urged her, by every consideration, to return; and we had reason to think, when she left our house, that she went back to you."

"Such is not the case," said Mr. Lane, with disappointment, and something of sadness in his tone. "I have not seen her since the morning of our unhappy difference. Where can she have gone?"

Mr. Edmondson was silent.

"Did she say that she was going to return home?" asked Mr. Lane.

"No. But we had reason to think that such was her intention. Have you heard nothing from her?"

"Not a word."

"It is strange!"

Mr. Lane heaved a deep sigh. A few more brief questions and answers passed, and then the two men separated. The forsaken husband went home with a sadder heart than he had yet known. The absence of his wife and child for several days—both objects of real affection—and absent under such peculiar and trying circumstances, had subdued, to a great extent, his angry feelings. He was prepared to yield much. He would even have gone to his wife, and acknowledged that he was partly in error, in order to have brought about a reconciliation. Something that she had said during their last, exciting interview, which he had rejected as untrue, or not causes of complaint, had represented themselves to his mind; and in the sober reflecting states that were predominant, he saw that he had not in all things treated her as an equal, nor regarded her at all times as possessing a rational freedom as independent as his own. Though he did not excuse her conduct, he yet thought of it less angrily than at first, and was willing to yield something in order to restore the old relations.

Anxiety and alarm now took possession of his mind. The distance between them had become wider, and the prospect of a reconciliation more remote. Amanda had gone, he could not tell whither. She had neither money nor friends; he knew not into what danger she might fall, nor what suffering she might encounter. It was plain from the manner of her leaving the house of Mr. Edmondson, that her resolution to remain away from him was fixed. He must, therefore, seek her out, and invite her to return. He must yield if he would reconcile this sad difficulty. And he was now willing to do so. But, where was she? Whither should he go in search of the wanderer?

The very means which her friend had taken to induce Mrs. Lane to return to her husband, had driven her farther away. The hint touching her husband's legal rights in the child, and his resolution to assert them, filled her with the deepest alarm, and determined her to put it beyond his power, if possible, to deprive her of the only thing in life to which her heart could now cling. Toward her husband, her feelings were those of an oppressed one for an oppressor. From the beginning, he had almost suffocated her own life by his pressure upon her freedom of will. She remembered, with, tears, his tenderness and his love; but soon would come the recollection of his constant interference in matters peculiarly her own; his evident contempt for her intellect; and his final efforts to subdue her rising independence, and make her little less than a domestic slave—and the fountain of her tears would become dry. Added to all this, was the fact of his resolution to recover his child by law. This crushed out all hope from her heart. He had no affection left for her. His love had changed to hate. He had assumed toward her the attitude of a persecutor. Nothing was now left for her but self-protection.

In leaving the home of her husband, Mrs. Lane had exercised no forethought. She made no estimate of consequences, and provided for no future contingencies. She was blind in her faint-heartedness, that was little less than despair. Any thing was better than to remain in a state of submission, that had become, she felt, intolerable. Leaving thus, Mrs. Lane had taken with her nothing beyond a few dollars in her purse, and it was only an accident that her purse was in her pocket. All her own clothes and those of her child, except what they had on, were left behind.

Alarmed at the threat of her husband, Mrs. Lane, a few hours after the conversation with Mrs. Edmondson, in which his views were made known to her, took her child and went away. In parting with her friend, she left upon her mind the impression that she was going home. This was very far from her intention. Her purpose was to leave New York, the city of her residence, as quickly as possible, and flee to some obscure village, where she would remain hidden from her husband. She had resided, some years before, for a short time in Philadelphia; and thither she resolved to go, and from thence reach some point in the country. On leaving the house of her friend, Mrs. Lane hurried to the river and took passage in the afternoon line for Philadelphia.

As the cars began their swift movement from Jersey City, a feeling of inexpressible sadness came over her, and she began to realize more distinctly than she had yet done, her desolate, destitute, and helpless condition. After paying her passage, she had only two dollars left in her purse; and, without money, how was she to gain friends and shelter in a strange city? To add to her unhappy feelings, her child commenced asking for her father.

"Where is papa?" she would repeat every few minutes. "I want to go to my papa."

This was continued until it ended in fretfulness and complaints at the separation it was enduring. Tears and sobs followed; and, finally, the child wept herself to sleep.

A new train of feelings was awakened by this incident. In leaving her husband, Mrs. Lane had thought only of herself. She had not once considered the effect of a separation from its father upon her child. Little Mary's heart was full of affection for the two beings whom nature prompted her to love. Her father's return from business had always been to her the happiest event of the day; and, when she sprang into his arms, her whole being would thrill with delight. Days had passed since she had seen her father, and she was pining to meet him again to lay her head upon his bosom—to feel his arms clasped tightly around her.

All this was realized by the mother, as the child lay sleeping on her arm, while the swift rolling cars bore them farther and farther away from the home she was leaving. Is it just to the child? Distinctly did this thought present itself in her mind. For a long time she mused over it, her feelings all the while growing more and more tender, until something like repentance for the step she had taken found its way into her mind—not for what she was herself suffering, but for the sake of her child. She had not thought of the effect upon little Mary, until the pain of absence showed itself in complaint.

This idea arose clearly before her—she could not push it aside; and, the more she pondered it, the more troubled did she become, from a new source. Would not the separation so deeply afflict the child as to rob her of all happiness?

While these thoughts had full possession of the mother's mind, Mary slept on and dreamed of her father, as was evident from the fact that, more than once, she murmured his name.

When night came down, its effect upon Mrs. Lane was more sadly depressing, for it brought her into a clearer realization of her unhappy condition. Where was she going? What was the uncertain future to bring forth? All was as dark as the night that had closed around her.

At length the cars reached Bristol, and it became necessary to leave them, and pass into the boat. In lifting Mary in her arms, to bear her from the cars, the child again murmured the name of her father, which so affected Mrs. Lane, that her tears gushed forth in spite of her efforts to restrain them. Letting her veil fall over her face to conceal this evidence of affliction from her fellow-passengers, she proceeded with the rest; and, in a little while, was gliding swiftly down the river. It was ten o'clock when they arrived in Philadelphia. For an hour previous to this time, the mind of the fugitive had been busy in the effort to determine what course she should take on gaining the end of her journey. But the nearer she came to its termination, the more confused did she become, and the less clearly did she see the way before her. Where should she go on reaching the city? There as no one to receive her; no one to whom she could go and claim protection, or even shelter.

This state of irresolution continued until the boat touched the wharf, and the passengers were leaving. Mary was awake again, and kept asking, every few moments, to go home.

"Yes, dear, we will go home," the mother would reply, in a tone of encouragement, while her own mind was in the greatest uncertainty and distress.

"Why don't papa come?" asked the child, as one after another moved away, and they were left standing almost alone. At this moment, an Irishman, with a whip in his hand, came up, and said—

"Want a carriage, ma'am?"

Mrs. Lane hesitated a moment or two, while she thought hurriedly, and then replied—

"Yes."

"Very well, ma'am; I'll attend to you. Where is your baggage?"

"I have only this basket with me."

"Ah! well; come along." And Mrs. Lane followed the man from the boat.

"Where shall I drive you?" he asked, after she had entered the carriage.

There was a pause, with apparent irresolution.

"I am a stranger here," said Mrs. Lane innocently. "I want to obtain pleasant accommodations for a day or two. Can you take me to a good place?"

"Faith, and I can—as good as the city will afford. Do you wish one of the tip-top places, where they charge a little fortune a week; or a good comfortable home at a reasonable price?"

"I want a comfortable, retired place, where the charges are not extravagant."

"Exactly; I understand."

And the driver closed the door, and, mounting his box, drove off. At the end of ten minutes the carriage stopped, the steps were let down, and Mrs. Lane, after descending, was shown into a small parlour, with dingy furniture. A broad, red-faced Irish woman soon appeared, at the summons of the driver.

"I've brought you a lady customer, Mrs. McGinnis, d'ye see? And you're just the one to make her at home and comfortable. She's a stranger, and wants a quiet place for a day or two."

"And, in troth, she'll find it here, as ye well say, John Murphy. Will the lady put off her bonnet? We'll have her room ready in a jiffy! Much obleeged to yees, John Murphy, for remembering us. What a darlint of a child; bless its little heart!"

"What must I pay you?" asked Mrs. Lane, hoarsely, turning to the driver.

"One dollar, ma'am," was replied.

Mrs. Lane drew forth her purse, towards which the Irishwoman glanced eagerly, and took therefrom the sum charged, and paid the man, who immediately retired. The landlady followed him out, and stood conversing with him at the door for several minutes. When she returned, she was less forward in her attentions to her guest, and somewhat inquisitive as to who she was, where she had come from, and whither she was going. All these Mrs. Lane evaded, and asked to have her room prepared as quickly as possible, as she did not feel very well, and wished to retire. The room was at length ready, and she went up with little Mary, who had again fallen to sleep. It was small, meagerly furnished, and offensive from want of cleanliness. In turning down the bed clothes, she found the sheets soiled and rumpled, showing that the linen had not been changed since being used by previous lodgers. The first thing that Mrs. Lane did, after laying her sleeping child upon the bed, was to sit down and weep bitterly. The difficulties about to invest her, as they drew nearer and nearer, became more and more apparent; and her heart sank and trembled as she looked at the unexpected forms they were assuming. But a single dollar remained in her purse; and she had an instinctive conviction that trouble with the landlady on account of money was before her. Had she been provided with the means of independence, she would have instantly called a servant, and demanded a better room, and fresh linen for her bed; but, under the circumstances, she dared not do this. She had a conviction that the Irishwoman was already aware of her poverty, and that any call for better accommodations would be met by insult. It was too late to seek for other lodgings, even if she knew where to go, and were not burdened with a sleeping child.

Unhappy fugitive! How new and unexpected were the difficulties that already surrounded her! How dark was the future! dark as that old Egyptian darkness that could be felt. As she sat and wept, the folly of which she was guilty in the step she had taken presented itself distinctly before her mind, and she wondered at her own blindness and want of forethought. Already, in her very first step, she had got her feet tangled. How she was to extricate them she could not see.

Wearied at last with grief and fear, her mind became exhausted with its own activity. Throwing herself upon the bed beside her child, without removing her clothes, she was soon lost in sleep. Daylight was stealing in, when the voice of little Mary awakened her.

"Where's papa?" asked the child, and she looked with such a sad earnestness into her mother's face, that the latter felt rebuked, and turned her eyes away from those of her child. "Want to go home," lisped the unhappy babe—"see papa."

"Yes, dear," soothingly answered the mother.

Little Mary turned her eyes to the door with an expectant look, as if she believed her father, whom she loved, was about to enter, and listened for some moments.

"Papa! papa!" she called in anxious tones, and listened again; but there was no response. Her little lip began to quiver, then it curled grievingly; and, falling over, she hid her face against her mother and began sobbing.

Tenderly did the mother take her weeping child to her bosom, and hold it there in a long embrace. After it had grown calm she arose, and adjusting her rumpled garments, and those of Mary, sat down by the windows to await the events that were to follow. In about half an hour a bell was rung in the passage below, and soon after a girl came to her room to say that breakfast was ready.

"I wish my breakfast brought to me here," said Mrs. Lane.

The girl stared a moment and then retired. Soon after, the Irish landlady made her appearance.

"What is it ye wants, mum?" said that personage, drawing herself up and assuming an air of vulgar dignity and importance.

"Nothing," replied Mrs. Lane, "except a little bread and milk for my child."

"Isn't yees coming down to breakfast?"

Mrs. Lane shook her head.

"Ye'd better. It's all ready."

"I don't wish any thing. But if you'll send me up something for my child, I will be obliged to you."

The landlady stood for some moments, as if undecided what she should do, and then retired. About half an hour afterwards, a dirty looking Irish girl appeared with a waiter, on which were the articles for which she had asked.

"Don't ye want any thing for yerself, mum?" asked the girl, with some kindness in her voice.

"No, I thank you," was replied.

"You'd better eat a little."

"I've no appetite," said Mrs. Lane, turning her face away to conceal the emotion that was rising to the surface.

The girl retired, and the food brought for the child was placed before her; but she felt as little inclined to eat as her mother, and could not be induced to take a mouthful. Turning from the offered food, she raised her tearful eyes to her mother's face, and in a choking voice said—"Go home, mamma—see papa."

The words smote, like heavy strokes, upon the mother's heart. How great a wrong had she done her child! But could she retrace her steps now? Could she go back and humble herself under the imperious will of her husband? Her heart shrunk from the thought. Any thing but that! it would crush the life out of her. An hour she sat, with these and kindred thoughts passing through her mind, when the girl who had brought up Mary's breakfast came in and said—"Won't yees walk down into the parlour, mum, while I clean up your room?"

"Is any one down there?" asked Mrs. Lane.

"No, mum," was answered by the girl.

With some reluctance Mrs. Lane descended to the small, dingy parlour, which she found adjoining a bar-room, whence there came the loud voices of men. From a window she looked forth upon the street, which was narrow, and crowded with carts, drays, and other vehicles. Opposite were old houses, in which business of various kinds was carried on. One was occupied by a cooper; another used as a storehouse for fish; another for a grog-shop. Every thing was dirty and crowded, and all appeared bustle and confusion. It was plain to her that she had fallen in an evil place, and that her first business must be escape. As she sat meditating upon the next step, there came suddenly, from the bar-room, the sound of angry voices, mingled with fierce threats and shocking blasphemy. Springing to her feet in terror, Mrs. Lane caught up her child, and was about starting from the door without any covering upon her head, when the landlady intercepted her.

"What's the matter with yees? Where are ye going?"

With quivering lips, and face white with alarm, Mrs. Lane replied—"Oh, ma'am! get me my things and let me go."

"Ye can go when ye pays yer bill, in welcome," replied the woman.

"How much is it?"

"It's a dollar and a half."

The Irishwoman looked steadily at Mrs. Lane, and saw, by the change in her countenance, what she had expected, that she had not as much money in her possession.

"Won't a dollar pay you?" asked Mrs. Lane, after standing with her eyes upon the floor for some moments. "I've had nothing but my night's lodging and surely a dollar will pay for that."

"Indade and it won't, then! Sure, and yer breakfast was got. If ye didn't ate it, I'm not to fault.

"Here is a dollar," said Mrs. Lane, taking out her purse. "I'm sure it's full pay for all I've received."

"And d'ye mane to call me an ould chate, ye spalpeen, ye!" indignantly replied the landlady, her face growing red with anger, while she raised her huge fist and shook it at her terrified guest, who retreated back into the parlour, and sank, trembling, into a chair.

"As if I wasn't an honest woman," continued the virago, following Mrs. Lane. "As if I'd extort on a lone woman! Give me patience! When ye pays the dollar and a half, ye can go; but not a foot shall ye take from my door until then."

A scuffle took place in the bar-room at that moment, attended by a new eruption of oaths and imprecations.

Quickly sprinting from her chair, Mrs. Lane, with Mary in her arms, glided from the room, and ran panting up-stairs to her chamber, the door of which she locked behind her on entering.

Half an hour of as calm reflection as it was possible for Mrs. Lane to make brought her to the resolution to leave the house at all hazards. Where she was to go, was to be an afterthought. The greatest evil was to remain; after escaping that, she would consider the means of avoiding what followed. Putting on her bonnet and shawl, and taking her basket, she went down-stairs with her child, determined, if possible, to get away unobserved, and after doing so, to send back, by any means that offered, the only dollar she possessed in the world to the landlady. No one met her on the stairs, and she passed the parlour-door unobserved. But, alas! the street-door was found locked and the key withdrawn. After a few ineffectual attempts to open it, Mrs. Lane went into the parlour, and, standing there, debated for some moments whether she should leave the house by passing through the bar-room, or wait for another opportunity to get away by the private entrance. While still bewildered and undetermined the landlady came in from the bar-room.

The moment she saw her guest, she comprehended the purpose in her mind.

"Where are ye going?" said she in a quick sharp voice, the blood rising to her coarse sensual face.

"I am going to leave your house," replied Mrs. Lane, in as firm a voice as she could command. As she spoke she drew forth her purse, and taking out the solitary dollar it contained, added—"Unfortunately, this is all the money I have with me, but I will send you the other half-dollar."

But the landlady refused to take the proffered money, and replied, indignantly,

"A purty how d'you do, indeed, to come into a genteel body's house, and then expect to get off without paying your bill. But ye don't know Biddy McGinnis—ye don't! If yees wants to go paceable, pay the dollar and a half. But until this is done, ye shall not cross my door-stone."

"I can't stay here! What good will it do?" said Mrs. Lane, wringing her hand. "It's all the money I've got; and remaining won't increase the sum, while it adds to the debt. Better let me go now."

"Indade, and ye'll not go, thin, my lady! I'll tache yees to come into a respectable body's house without as much money in yer pocket as 'll pay for the night's lodging. I wonder who ye are, any how! No better than ye should be, I'll warrint!"

While speaking, the Irishwoman had drawn nearer and nearer, and now stood with her face only a few inches from that of her distressed guest, who, bursting into tears, clasped her hands together, and sobbed—

"Let me go! let me go! If you have the heart of a woman, let me go!"

"Heart of a woman, indade!" returned Mrs. McGinnis, indignantly. "Yer a purty one to talk to me about the heart of a woman. Stalein into a body's house at twelve o'clock at night, and thin tryin' to go off without paying for the lodgings and breakfast. Purty doings!"

"What's the matter here?" said a well dressed man, stepping in from the bar-room and closing the door behind him. "What do you mean by talking to the lady in this way, Mrs. McGinnis? I've been listening to you."

There was an instant change in the Irishwoman. Her countenance fell, and she retreated a few steps from the object of her vituperation.

"What's all this about? I should like to know," added the man in a decided way. "Will you explain, madam?" addressing Mrs. Lane, in a kind voice. "But you are agitated. Sit down and compose yourself."

"Let her pay me my money, that's all I want," muttered the landlady.

In a moment the man's purse was drawn from his pocket. "What does she owe you?"

"A dollar and a half, bad luck till her!"

"There's your money, you old termagant!" And the man handed her the amount. "And now, as you are paid, and have nothing more to say to this lady, please to retire and let her be freed from your presence."

"Yees needint call me ill names, Misther Bond," said the woman, in a subdued voice, as she retired. "It doesn't become a jentilman like you. I didn't mane any harm. I only wanted my own, and sure I've a right to that."

"Well, you've got your own, though not in a way that does either you or your house much credit," returned the man. "The next time you are so fortunate as to get a lady in your hotel, I hope you'll know better how to treat her."

Mrs. McGinnis retired without further remark, and the man turned to Mrs. Lane, and said, in a kind, respectful manner,

"I am sorry to find you so unhappily situated, and will do any thing in my power to relieve you from your present embarrassment. Your landlady here is a perfect virago. How did you happen to fall into her hands?"

Encouraged by the kindness of the man's address, as well as from the fact that he had rescued her from a violent woman, Mrs. Lane, after composing herself, said—

"I came in from New York last night, and, being a stranger, asked the cabman to take me to a good hotel. He brought me here. I happened to have but two dollars in my purse, he charged one for carriage hire."

"The extortioner!"

"Finding into what a wretched place he had brought me, I wished to leave this morning, but have been prevented because I could not pay a dollar and a half when I had only a dollar. I told her to let me go, and I would send her the balance claimed; but she only met the proposition by insult."

"The wretch!" exclaimed the man, indignantly. "I happened to be passing, and, hearing her loud voice, glanced in at the window. In an instant I comprehended, to some extent, the difficulty; and, knowing her of old, came in to see if something were not wrong. She is a bad woman, and her house is a snare for the innocent. It is fortunate for you that I came at the right moment!"

Mrs. Lane shuddered.

"And now, madam," said the man, "what can I do for you? Have you friends in the city?"

"I am an entire stranger here," replied Mrs. Lane.

"Were you going farther?

"Yes," was answered after some hesitation.

"Where do your friends reside?"

"In New York."

"Ah!"

"This is your child?" was said, after a pause.

"Yes."

There was something in the man's manner, and in the way he looked at her, that now made Mrs. Lane shrink from, as instinctively as she had at first leaned towards him. Beneath his steady eye her own drooped and rested for some moments on the floor.

"Is your husband in New York?" pursued the man.

This question caused the heart of Mrs. Lane to bound with a sudden throb. Her husband! She had deserted him, her natural and lawful protector, and already she was encompassed with difficulties and surrounded by dangers. What would she not at that moment have given to be safely back in the home she had left? To the last question she gave a simple affirmative.

"Where do you wish to go when you leave here?" inquired the man, who had perceived a change in her and understood its nature.

"I wish to be taken to a good hotel, where I can remain a day or two, until I have time to communicate with my friends. My being out of money is owing to an inadvertence. I will receive a supply immediately on writing home."

The man drew his purse from his pocket, and, presenting it, said—

"This is at your service. Take whatever you need."

Mrs. Lane thanked him, but drew back.

"Only get me into some safe place, until I can write to my friends," said she, "and you would lay both them and me under the deepest obligations."

The man arose at this, and stepping into the bar room, desired the barkeeper to send for a carriage. From a stand near by one was called. When it came to the door, he informed Mrs. Lane of the fact, and asked if she were ready to go.

"Where will you take me?" she asked.

"To the United States Hotel," replied the man. "You could not be in a safer or better place."

On hearing this, Mrs. Lane arose without hesitation, and, going from the house, entered the carriage with the man, and was driven away. Drawing her veil over her face, she shrank into a corner of the vehicle, and remained in sad communion with her own thoughts for many minutes. From this state of abstraction, the stopping of the carriage aroused her. The driver left his seat and opened the door, when her companion stepped forth, saying as he did so—

"This is the place," and offering at the same time his hand.

As Mrs. Lane descended to the street, she glanced with a look of anxious inquiry around her. Already a suspicion that all might not be right was disturbing her mind. Two years before she had been in Philadelphia, and had stayed several days at the United States Hotel. She remembered the appearance of the building and the street, but now she did not recognise a single object. All was strange.

"Is this the United States Hotel?" she asked eagerly.

"Oh, yes, ma'am," was the smiling reply. "We are at the private entrance."

Her bewildered mind was momentarily deceived by this answer, and she permitted herself to be led into a house, which she soon discovered not to be an hotel. The most dreadful suspicions instantly seized her. So soon as she was shown into a parlour, the man retired. A woman came in shortly afterwards, who, from her appearance, seemed to be the mistress of the house. She spoke kindly to Mrs. Lane, and asked if she would walk up into her room.

"There has been some mistake," said the poor wanderer, her lips quivering in spite of her efforts to assume a firm exterior.

"Oh, no, none at all," quickly replied the woman, smiling.

"Yes, yes there is. I am not in the hotel where I wished to go. Why have I been brought here? Where is the man with whom I came?"

"He has gone away; but will return again. In the mean time do not causelessly distress yourself. You are safe from all harm."

"But I am not where I wished to go," replied Mrs. Lane. "Will you be kind enough to give me the direction of the United States Hotel, and I will walk there with my child."

The woman shook her head.

"I could not permit you to go until Mr. Bond returned," said she. "He brought you here, and will expect to find you when he comes back."

"I will not remain." And as she said this in a firm voice, Mrs. Lane arose, and, taking her little girl in her arms, made an attempt to move through the door into the passage. But the woman stepped before her quickly, and in a mild, yet decided way, told her that she could not leave the house.

"Why not?" asked the trembling creature.

"Mr. Bond has placed you in my care, and will expect to find you on his return," answered the woman.

"Who is Mr. Bond? What right has he to control my movements?"

"Did you not place yourself in his care?" inquired the woman. "I understood him to say that such was the case."

"He offered to protect me from wrong and insult."

"And, having undertaken to do so, he feels himself responsible to your friends for your safe return to their hands. I am responsible to him."

"Deceived! deceived! deceived!" murmured Mrs. Lane, bursting into tears and sinking into a chair, while she hugged her child tightly in her arms, and laid its face against her own.

The woman seemed slightly moved at this exhibition of distress, and stood looking at the quivering frame of the unhappy fugitive, with a slight expression of regret on her face. After Mrs. Lane had grown calm, the woman said to her:

"Is your husband living?"

"He is," was answered, in a steady voice.

"Where does he reside?" continued the woman.

"In New York," replied Mrs. Lane.

"What is his name?"

Mrs. Lane reflected, hurriedly, for some moments, and then gave a correct answer, adding, at the same time, that for any attempted wrong, there would come a speedy and severe retribution. The next inquiry of the woman was as to her husband's occupation, which was also answered correctly.

"And now," added Mrs. Lane, with assumed firmness, "you had better let me retire from this place immediately, and thus avoid trouble, which, otherwise, you would be certain to have. My husband is a merchant of influence, and a man who will not stop at half measures in seeking to redress a wrong. This man, whoever he may be, who has so basely deceived me, will find, ere long, that he has done an act which will hot go unpunished, and that severely. As for yourself, be warned in time, and let me go from this place."

Again Mrs. Lane sought to pass from the room, but was prevented. The woman was neither harsh, rude, nor insulting in her manner, but firmly refused to let her leave the house, saying—"I am responsible for your safe keeping, and cannot, therefore, let you go."

She then urged her to go up-stairs and lay off her things, but Mrs. Lane refused, in the most positive manner, to leave the parlour.

"You will be more comfortable in the chamber we have prepared for you," said the woman, coldly; "but you must do as you like. If you want any thing, you can ring for it."

And saying this, she turned from the room, and locked the door through which she retired. The instant she was gone, Mrs. Lane sprang towards one of the front windows, threw it up and attempted to draw the bolt which fastened the shutter; but her effort was not successful: the bolt remained immovable. On a closer inspection, she found that it was locked. The back window was open, but a glance into the yard satisfied her that it would be useless to attempt escape in that way. Hopeless in mind and paralyzed in body, she again sank down inactive.

Little Mary, who had been left standing on the floor during this effort to escape, now came up to where she had thrown herself upon a sofa, and, laying her little face upon her breast, looked tearfully at her, and said, in a low, sorrowful voice—"Won't papa come? I want my papa—my dear papa."

Not a word could the mother reply to her unhappy child, who, in her folly, she had so wronged. Oh, what would she not have given at that moment to see the face of her husband!

Five or six hours had passed. In a small sitting room, near the parlour in which Mrs. Lane was still a prisoner, stood the man named Bond, and the woman who had received her.

"Mrs. Lane did you say she called herself?" said the man, with a sudden change of manner—"and from New York?"

"Yes."

"Did you inquire her husband's business?"

"She said he was a merchant of standing, and threatened both you and me with the severest consequences, if she were not instantly released."

"Can it be possible!" remarked the man, and he stood in a musing attitude for some time. "I'm a little afraid this affair is not going to turn out quite so pleasantly as I at first supposed. I think I know her husband."

"You do!"

"Yes. We have had several business transactions together, if he is the individual I suppose him to be."

"Then you had better get her off of your hands as quickly as possible; and this will be no hard matter. Only open the cage-door, and the bird will fly."

"Confound that Irish huzzy! She and her John Murphy have scared up a nice bit of adventure for me."

"Both you and they ought to have known better than to expect any thing but trouble from a woman with a baby. As it is, the best thing for you is to get her off of your hands forthwith."

"I don't like to give up after progressing so far. It isn't my disposition."

"A wise man foresees evil, and gets out of its way."

"True; and my better course is to step aside, I suppose. But what shall we do with her?"

"Open the cage-door, as I said, and let her escape."

"Where will she go?"

"Have you any concern on that head?"

"Some. Moreover, I don't just comprehend the meaning of her visit here alone at night, and without money. I wonder if, after all, there isn't a lover in the case, who has failed to meet her."

"Most likely," returned the woman.

"In that event, why may not I take his place?"

"It will require her consent. Better have nothing more to do with her, and thus keep out of the way of trouble.

"Her husband, if she be the wife of the man I think she is," said Bond, "will hardly stop at half-way measures in an affair like this."

"So much the more reason for keeping out of his way."

"Perhaps so; and yet I like adventure, especially when spiced with a little danger. Upon second thought, I'll let her remain here until to-morrow."

"Just as you like. But I've been unable to get her up-stairs; and she can't stay in the parlour all night."

"No. She must go to the chamber you have prepared for her."

"How will we get her there?"

"Use every effort you can to induce her to comply with our wishes in this respect. I will come in after nightfall, and, if you have not been successful, will remove her by force."

With this understanding, the partners in evil separated.

Soon after parting with Mr. Edmondson, who had informed Mr. Lane that his wife was no longer at his house, and when the latter had begun to feel exceedingly anxious, he met a gentleman who said to him, "When do you expect Mrs. Lane back?"

It was with difficulty that the deserted husband could refrain from the exhibition of undue surprise at such an unexpected question.

"I was over the river yesterday afternoon with a friend who was on his way to Philadelphia," added the man, "and saw your lady in the cars."

"Good morning," said Mr. Lane, as he looked at his watch, and then turned away with a hurried manner.

It was half-past eleven o'clock. At twelve a line started for the South. Lane was on board the steamboat when it left the dock. Six hours and a half of most intense anxiety were passed ere the unhappy man reached Philadelphia. On arriving, he took a carriage and visited all the principal hotels, but not a word could he hear of his wife. He then bethought him to make some inquiries of the hackman whom he had employed.

"Were you at the wharf last night when the New York line came in?" he asked, as he stood with his hand on the carriage-door, after leaving one of the hotels, again disappointed in his search.

"I was," replied the hackman.

"Did you get any passengers?"

"No, sir."

"Did you see any thing of a lady with a child?"

The hackman thought for a little while, and then replied—

"Yes, I did. There was a lady and a child, nearly the last on the boat. John Murphy drove them away."

"Where can I find John Murphy?" eagerly enquired Mr. Lane.

"He's probably on the stand."

"Drive me there if you please." And he sprang into the carriage.

In a few minutes they were at a carriage stand; and Mr. Lane heard the driver call out, as he reined up his horses—"Hallo! there, John Murphy! here's a gentleman who wants to see you."

The person addressed came up as Mr. Lane descended from the carriage.

"I understand," said Lane, "that you received a lady and child in your carriage, last night, from the New York line. Where did you take them?"

"Who said that I did?" boldly inquired the man addressed.

"I said so!" as firmly replied the driver who had given the information to Mr. Lane. "What interest have you in denying it?"

Murphy evinced some surprise at this, and looked a little dashed, but repeated his denial.

A new fear instantly seized Mr. Lane. His wife might have been entrapped into some den of infamy, through means of the driver she had employed to convey her to an hotel. The thought affected him like an electric shock.

"You are certain of what you say?" asked Mr. Lane, turning to the hackman he had employed.

"Certain," was answered positively.

"Is there a police officer near at hand?" was the next inquiry. This was intended as no threat; and Murphy understood its meaning.

The eyes of Mr. Lane were fixed on his face, and he saw in it a guilty change. No reply being made to the question about a police officer, Mr. Lane said, addressing the accused hackman—

"If you wish to escape trouble, take me instantly to the house where I can find the lady you took from the boat last night. She is my wife, and I will go through fire and water to find her; and let him who stands in my way take the consequences."

Murphy now drew Mr. Lane aside, and said a few words to him hurriedly.

"Can I depend upon what you say?" eagerly asked the latter.

"Yes, upon honour!" replied the hackman.

"You must go with me," said Lane.

"I cannot leave the stand."

"I will call a policeman and compel you to go with me, if you don't accompany me peaceably. As I live, I will not part from you until I find her! Take your choice—go quietly, or under compulsion."

There was a fierce energy in the excited man that completely subdued the Irish hackman, who, after a further, though feeble remonstrance, got into the carriage with Mr. Lane, and was driven off. The course taken was out— street. Some distance beyond Washington Square, the carriage stopped before a house, in which Mr. Lane was informed that he would find the woman whom Murphy had taken from the boat the night before. He stepped out quickly, and, as he sprang across the pavement, Murphy, who was out of the carriage almost as soon as he was, glided around the corner of a street, and was beyond recall. A quick jerk of the bell was answered by a female servant, who held the door only partly open, while Lane addressed her.

"Wasn't there a woman and child brought here last night?" said he, in an agitated manner.

"No, sir," replied the girl; and, as she spoke, she made an attempt to close the door, seeing which, Mr. Lane thrust a part of his body in and prevented the movement.

"Are you certain?" he asked.

"I am," was positively answered, while the girl strove to shut the door by forcing it against Mr. Lane. At this moment something like a smothered cry from within reached his ears, when, throwing open the door with a sudden application of strength that prostrated the girl, he stepped over her body and entered the vestibule. Just then there arose a wild cry for help! He knew the voice; it came from one of the parlours, into which he rushed. There he saw his wife struggling in the arms of a woman and a man, while his frightened child stood near, white and speechless with terror. As he entered, Amanda saw him.

"Oh, my husband!" she exclaimed. In a moment she was released, and the man and woman fled from the room, but not before the face of the former was fully recognised by Mr. Lane.

Little Mary had already sprung to her father, and was quivering and panting on his breast.

"Oh! take me away quickly—quickly!" cried Mrs. Lane, staggering towards her husband and falling into his arms.

Without waiting for explanations, Mr. Lane went from the house with his wife and child, and, placing them in the carriage at the door, was driven to an hotel.

The reader doubtless understands the scene we have just described. The man named Bond was in the act of carrying out his threat to remove Mrs. Lane to a chamber by force when her husband appeared.

Of all that passed between the severely-tried husband and wife after their meeting, it behooves us not to write. The circumstances we have detailed were exceedingly painful to the parties most interested; but their effect, like the surgeon's knife, was salutary. Mr. Lane afterwards regarded his wife from an entirely different point of view, and found her a very different woman from what he had at first believed her to be. He saw in her a strength of character and a clearness of intellect for which he had never given her credit; and, from looking down upon her as a child or an inferior, came to feel towards her as an equal.

His indignation at the treatment she had received in Philadelphia was extreme. The man named Bond he knew very well, and he at first determined to call him to account personally; but as this would lead to a mortifying notoriety and exposure of the whole affair, he was reluctantly induced to keep silence. Bond has never crossed his way since: it might not be well for him to do so.

Some years have passed. No one who meets Mr. and Mrs. Lane, at home or abroad, would dream that, at one time, they were driven asunder by a strong repulsion. Few are more deeply attached, or happier in their domestic relations; but neither trespasses on the other's rights, nor interferes with the other's prerogative. Mutual deference, confidence, respect, and love, unite them with a bond that cannot again be broken.

THE INVALID WIFE.

"MY poor head! It seems as if it would burst!" murmured Mrs. Bain, as she arose from a stooping position, and clasped her temples with both hands. She was engaged in dressing a restless, fretful child, some two or three years old. Two children had been washed and dressed, and this was the last to be made ready for breakfast.

As Mrs. Bain stood, with pale face, closed eyes, and tightly compressed lips, still clasping her throbbing temples, the bell announcing the morning meal was rung. The sound caused her to start, and she said, in a low and fretful voice—

"There's the breakfast bell; and Charley isn't ready yet; nor have I combed my hair. How my head does ache! I am almost blind with the pain."

Then she resumed her work of dressing Charley, who struggled, cried, and resisted, until she was done.

Mr. Bain was already up and dressed. He was seated in the parlour, enjoying his morning paper, when the breakfast bell rang. The moment he heard the sound, he threw down his newspaper, and, leaving the parlour, ascended to the dining-room. His two oldest children were there, ready to take their places at the table.

"Where's your mother?" he inquired of one of them.

"She's dressing Charley," was answered.

"Never ready in time," said Mr. Bain, to himself, impatiently. He spoke in an under tone.

For a few moments he stood with his hands on the back of his chair. Then he walked twice the length of the dining-room; and then he went to the door and called—

"Jane! Jane! Breakfast is on the table."

"I'll be there in a minute," was replied by Mrs. Bain.

"Oh, yes! I know something about your minutes." Mr. Bain said this to himself. "This never being in time annoys me terribly. I'm always ready. I'm always up to time. But there's no regard to time in this house."

Mrs. Bain was still struggling with her cross and troublesome child, when the voice of her impatient husband reached her. The sound caused a throb of intenser pain to pass through her aching head.

"Jane, make haste! Breakfast is all getting cold, and I'm in a hurry to go away to business," was called once more.

"Do have a little patience. I'll be there in a moment," replied Mrs. Bain.

"A moment! This is always the way."

And Mr. Bain once more paced backwards and forwards.

Meantime the wife hurriedly completed her own toilet, and then repaired to the dining-room. She was just five minutes too late.

One glance at her pale, suffering face should have changed to sympathy and pity the ill-humour of her thoughtless, impatient husband. But it was not so. The moment she appeared, he said—

"This is too bad, Jane! I've told you, over and over, that I don't like to wait after the bell rings. My mother was always promptly at her place, and

I'd like my wife to imitate so good an example."

Perhaps nothing could have hurt Mrs. Bain more than such a cruel reference of her husband to his mother, coupled with so unfeeling a declaration of his will concerning her—as if she were to be the mere creature of his will.

A sharp reply was on the tongue of Mrs. Bain; but she kept it back. The pain in her head subsided all at once; but a weight and oppression in her breast followed that was almost suffocating.

Mr. Bain drank his coffee, and eat his steak and toast, with a pretty fair relish; for he had a good appetite and a good digestion—and was in a state of robust health. But Mrs. Bain ate nothing. How could she eat? And yet, it is but the truth to say, that her husband, who noticed the fact, attributed her abstinence from food more to temper than want of appetite. He was aware that he had spoken too freely, and attributed the consequent change in his wife's manner to anger rather than a wounded spirit.

"Do you want any thing?" asked Mr. Bain, on rising from the table and turning to leave the room. He spoke with more kindness than previously.

"No," was the wife's brief answer, made without lifting her eyes to her husband's face.

"In the sulks!"

Mr. Bain did not say this aloud, but such was his thought, as he turned away and left the house. He did not feel altogether comfortable, of course. No man feels comfortable while there is a cloud upon the brow of his wife, whether it be occasioned by peevishness, ill-temper, bodily or mental suffering. No, Mr. Bain did not feel altogether comfortable, nor satisfied with himself, as he walked along to his store; for there came across his mind a dim recollection of having heard the baby fretting and crying during the night; and also of having seen the form of his wife moving to and fro in the chamber, while he lay snugly reposing in bed.

But these were unpleasant images, and Mr. Bain thrust them from his mind.

While Mr. Bain took his morning walk to his store, his lungs freely and pleasurably expanding in the pure, invigorating air, his wife, to whose throbbing temples the anguish had returned, and whose relaxed muscles had scarcely enough tension to support the weight of her slender frame, slowly and painfully began the work of getting her two oldest children ready for school. This done, the baby had to be washed and dressed. It screamed during the whole operation, and when, at last, it fell asleep upon her bosom, she was so completely exhausted, that she had to lie down. Tears wet her pillow as she lay with her babe upon her arm. He, to whom alone she had a right to look for sympathy, for support, and for strength in her many trials, did not appear to sympathize with her in the least. If she looked sober from the pressure of pain, fatigue, or domestic trials, he became impatient, and sometimes said, with cruel thoughtlessness, that he was tired of clouds and rain, and would give the world for a wife who could smile now and then. If, amid her many household cares and duties, she happened to neglect some little matter that affected his comfort, he failed not to express his annoyance, and not always in carefully chosen words. No wonder that her woman's heart melted—no wonder that hot tears were on her cheeks.

Mr. Bain had, as we have said, an excellent appetite; and he took especial pleasure in its gratification. He liked his dinner particularly, and his dinners were always good dinners. He went to market himself. On his way to his store he passed through the market, and his butcher sent home what he purchased.

"The marketing has come home," said the cook to Mrs. Bain, about ten o'clock, arousing her from a brief slumber into which she had fallen—a slumber that exhausted nature demanded, and which would have done far more than medicine for the restoration of something like a healthy tone to her system.

"Very well. I will come down in a little while," returned Mrs. Bain, raising herself on her elbow, and see about dinner. "What has Mr. Bain sent home?"

"A calf's head."

"What!"

"A calf's head."

"Very well. I will be down to see about it." Mrs. Bain repressed any further remark.

Sick and exhausted as she felt, she must spend at least two hours in the kitchen in making soup and dressing the calf's head for her husband's dinner. Nothing of this could be trusted to the cook, for to trust any part of its preparation to her was to have it spoiled.

With a sigh, Mrs. Bain arose from the bed. At first she staggered across the room like one intoxicated, and the pain, which had subsided during her brief slumber, returned again with added violence. But, really sick as she felt, she went down to the kitchen and passed full two hours there in the preparation of delicacies for her husband's dinner. And what was her reward?

"This is the worst calf's head soup you ever made. What have you done to it?" said Mr. Bain, pushing the plate of soup from before him, with an expression of disgust on his face.

There were tears in the eyes of the suffering wife, and she lifted them to her husband's countenance. Steadily she looked at him for a few moments; then her lips quivered, and the tears fell over her cheeks. Hastily rising, she left the dining room.

"It is rather hard that I can't speak without having a scene," muttered Mr. Bain, as he tried his soup once more. It did not suit his taste at all; so he pushed it from him, and made his dinner of something else.

As his wife had been pleased to go off up-stairs in a huff, just at a word, Mr. Bain did not feel inclined to humour her. So, after finishing his dinner, he took his hat and left the house, without so much as seeking to offer a soothing word.

Does the reader wonder that, when Mr. Bain returned in the evening, he found his wife so seriously ill as to make it necessary to send for their family physician? No, the reader will not wonder at this.

But Mr. Bain felt a little surprised. He had not anticipated any thing of the kind.

Mrs. Bain was not only ill, but delirious. Her feeble frame, exhausted by maternal duties, and ever-beginning, never-ending household cares, had yielded under the accumulation of burdens too heavy to bear.

For a while after Mr. Bain's return, his wife talked much, but incoherently; then she became quiet. But her fever remained high, and inflammation tended strongly towards the brain. He was sitting by the bedside about ten o'clock, alone with her, when she began to talk in her wandering way again; but her words were distinct and coherent.

"I tried to do it right," said she, sadly; "but my head ached so that I did not know what I was doing. Ah me! I never please him now in any thing. I wish I could always look pleasant—cheerful. But I can't. Well! well! it won't last for ever. I never feel well—never—never—never! And I'm so faint and weak in the morning! But he has no patience with me. *He* doesn't know what it is to feel sick. Ah me!"

And her voice sighed itself away into silence.

With what a rebuking force did these words fall upon the ears of Mr. Bain! He saw himself in a new light. He was the domestic tyrant, and not the kind and thoughtful husband.

A few days, and Mrs. Bain was moving about her house and among her children once more, pale as a shadow, and with lines of pain upon her forehead. How differently was she now treated by her husband! With what considerate tenderness he regarded her! But, alas! he saw his error too late! The gentle, loving creature, who had come to his side ten years before, was not much longer to remain with him. A few brief summers came and went, and then her frail body was laid amid the clods of the valley.

Alas! how many, like Mrs. Bain, have thus passed away, who, if truly loved and cared for, would have been the light of now darkened hearths, and the blessing and joy of now motherless children and bereaved husbands!

THE FIRST AND LAST QUARREL.

"IF I am his wife, I am not his slave!" said young Mrs. Huntley, indignantly. "It was more than he dared do a month ago."

"If you love me, Esther, don't talk in this way," said Mrs. Carlisle.

"Am I his slave aunt?" and the young bride drew herself up, while her eyes flashed.

"No, Esther, you are his wife."

"To be loved, and not commanded! That is the difference, and he has got to learn it."

"Were Edward to see and hear you now, do you think your words, manner, and expression would inspire him with any new affection for you?"

"I have nothing to do with that. I only express a just indignation, and that is a right I did not alienate when I consented to become his wife."

"You are a silly girl, Esther," said Mrs. Carlisle, "and I am afraid will pay dear for your folly. Edward has faults, and so have you. If you understood the duties and responsibilities of your position, and felt the true force of your marriage vows, you would seek to bend into better forms the crooked branches of your husband's hereditary temper, rather than commit an irreparable injury by roughly breaking them. I was not pleased with Edward's manner of speaking; but I must admit that he had provocation: that you were first, and, therefore, most to blame."

"I objected to going with him to the opera, because I particularly wanted to call and see Anna Lewis to-night. I had made up my mind to this, and when I make up my mind to any thing I do not like to be turned from my purpose."

"Edward resembles you rather too much in that respect. Therefore, there must be a disposition to yielding and self-denial on one side or the other, or unhappiness will follow. Hitherto, as far as I have been able to see, the yielding has all been on the part of Edward, who has given up to you in everything. And now, when he shows that he has a will of his own, you become very indignant, and talk bout not being his slave."

"It is too bad for you to speak so, aunt! You never think I do any thing right." And Esther burst into tears.

Meantime, Edward Huntley, the husband, was at the opera, listening to, but not enjoying, the beauties Norma. It was only a month since he had led to the altar his beautiful bride, and felt himself the happiest man in the world. Before marriage, he thought only of how he should please Esther. The preference of his own wishes to hers was felt as no sacrifice. But, after the hymeneal contract had been gratified, his feelings began gradually to change. What he had yielded in kindness was virtually demanded as a right, and against this, the moment it was perceived, his spirit rose in rebellion. In several instances, he gave way to what savoured, much more than he liked, of imperiousness.

Norma had just been brought out, and received with unprecedented favour. The newspapers were filled with its praises, and the beauties of the opera were spoken of by every one. A friend lauded it with more than usual enthusiasm, on the day it was advertised for a third performance.

"You haven't heard it yet!" said he, with surprise, on learning that Huntley had yet to enjoy that pleasure.

"No, but I think I will buy tickets for to-night."

"Do by all means! And get them at once, or you will not be able to secure a seat."

It was in the afternoon, and Huntley could not ask his young wife about it, unless he made a special errand home, which, as he lived some distance away from his office, would be inconvenient. Not in the least doubting, however, that Esther would be pleased to go to the opera, as she had more than once expressed a wish to see and hear Norma, he secured tickets and considered the matter settled.

Now that the gratification of hearing the opera was so near at hand, Huntley kept thinking of the enjoyment he was to have, and wishing for the time to pass more rapidly. He pictured, too, the pleasure that Esther would feel and express when she found that he had procured tickets. Half an hour earlier than usual he was at home. He found Esther and her aunt, Mrs. Carlisle, with whom they were living, in the parlour.

"We are going to see Norma to-night," said Huntley, in a gay voice, and with a broad smile upon his face, as he sat down beside Esther and took her hand.

"*We* are?"

The tone and look with which this was said chilled the warm feelings of the young man.

"*I* am, at least," said he, in a changed voice.

"And *I* am not," as promptly, and much more decidedly, replied Esther.

"Oh, yes you are." This was said with a suddenly assumed, half playful, yet earnest manner. "I have bought tickets, and we will go to-night."

"The least you could have done was to have asked me before you bought tickets," returned Esther. "I wish to go somewhere else to-night."

"But, as I have the tickets now, you will go, of course. To-morrow night will do as well for a visit."

"I wish to make it to-night."

"Esther, you are unreasonable." Huntley knit his brows and compressed his lips.

"We are quite even then." The pretty lip of the bride curled.

"Esther!" said Huntley, assuming a calm but cold exterior, and speaking in a firm voice. "I have bought tickets for the opera to-night, thinking that to go would give you pleasure, and now my wish is that you accompany me."

"A wish that you will certainly not have gratified. I believe I am your wife, not your slave to command."

There was something so cutting in the way this was said, that Huntley could not bear it. Without a word he arose, and, taking his hat, left the house. In a fever of excitement he walked the street for an hour and a half, and then, scarcely reflecting upon what he did, went to the opera. But the music was discord in his ears, and he left before the performance was half over.

The moment Esther heard the street-door close upon her husband, she arose and went from the room where she was sitting with her aunt, moving erect and with a firm step. Mrs. Carlisle did not see her for two hours. The tea bell rang, but she did not come down from her chamber, where, as the aunt supposed, she was bitterly repenting what she had done. In this, however, she was mistaken, as was proved, when, on joining her in her room for the purpose of striving to console her, the conversation with which our story opens took place.

When the fit of weeping with which Esther received the reproof her aunt felt called upon to give, had subsided, Mrs. Carlisle said, in a most solemn and impressive manner,

"What has occurred this evening may prove the saddest event of your whole life. There is no calculating the result. No matter whose the fault, the consequences that follow may be alike disastrous to the happiness of both. Are you prepared, thus early, for a sundering of the sacred bonds that have united you? And yet, even this may follow. It has followed with others, and may follow with you. Oh! the consequences of a first quarrel! Who can anticipate them?"

The voice of Mrs. Carlisle trembled, and then sank almost into a sob. Her manner more than her words startled Esther.

"What do you mean, aunt?" said she.

But her aunt was too much disturbed to speak for some minutes.

"Esther," she at length said, speaking in a voice that still trembled, "I knew a girl, who, at your age, married an excellent, but proud-spirited young man. Like Edward, the lover yielded too much when, as the husband, he began to be a little less considerate, and to act as if he had a will of his own, his wife set herself against him just as you set yourself against Edward. This chafed him, although he strove to conceal his feelings. But, in an unguarded moment, when his young wife was unusually self-willed, a quarrel of no more serious character than the one that has occurred this evening, between you and Edward, took place. They parted in anger as you parted, and—"

The aunt was unable for some time to control her voice sufficiently to finish the sentence—

"And never met again," she at length said, with such visible emotion as betrayed more than she had wished to reveal.

"Never met again!" ejaculated Esther, a sudden fear trembling through her heart, and causing her cheeks to grow pale.

"Never!" was the solemn response.

"Why, dear aunt? Why?" eagerly inquired Esther.

"Pride caused him," said Mrs. Carlisle, recovering her self-possession, "after a breach had been made, to leave not only his home, but the city in which he lived. Repenting of her ungenerous contact, his bride waited anxiously for his return at evening, but waited it vain. Sadly enough passed the lonely hours of that dreadful night, and morning found her a sleepless watcher. Days passed, but no word came from the unhappy wanderer from home and love. A week, and still all was silence and mystery. At the end of that time a letter was received from a neighbouring city, which brought intelligence to his friends that he was there, and lying dangerously ill. By the next conveyance his almost frantic wife started for the purpose of joining him. Alas! she was too late. When she stood beside the bed upon which he lay, she looked only upon the inanimate form of her husband. Death had been there before her. Esther! thirty years have passed since then, but the anguish I felt when I stood and looked upon the cold, dead, face of my husband, in that terrible hour, time has not altogether obliterated!"

Esther had risen to her feet, and now stood with her pale lips parted, and her cheeks blanched to an ashy whiteness.

"Dear aunt is all this true?" she asked huskily, while she grasped the arm of her relative.

"Heaven knows it is too true, my child! It was the first and, the last quarrel I had with my husband. And now, as you value your own and Edward's peace of mind, be warned by my sad example, and let the present unhappy difference that has occurred be quickly reconciled. Acknowledge your error the moment you see him, and make a firm resolution that you will, under no circumstances, permit the slightest misunderstanding again to take place. Yield to him, and you will find him ready as before to yield to you. What he was not ready to give under the force of a demand, love will prompt him cheerfully to render."

"Oh! if Edward should never return!" Esther said, clasping her hands together. She had scarcely heard the last sentence of her aunt.

"You need not fear on that account, my child," replied Mrs. Carlisle, in a voice meant to inspire confidence. "Edward will no doubt return. Few men act so rashly as to separate themselves at the first misunderstanding, although, too often, the first quarrel is but the prelude to others of a more violent kind, that end in severing the most sacred of all bonds, or rendering the life that might have been one of the purest felicity, an existence of misery. When Edward comes home to-night, forget every thing but your own error, and freely confess that. Then, all will be sunshine in a moment, although the light will fall and sparkle upon dewy tear-drops."

"I was mad to treat him so!" was Esther's response to this, as she paced the floor, with uneasy step. "Oh! if he should never return."

Once possessed with the idea that he would not return, the poor wife was in an agony of fear. No suggestion made by her aunt in the least relieved her mind. One thought—one fear—absorbed every thing else. Thus passed the evening, until ten o'clock came. From that time Esther began to listen anxiously for her husband's return, but hour after hour went by, and she was still a tearful watcher.

"I shall go mad if I sit here any longer!" murmured Huntley to himself, as the music came rushing upon his agitated soul, in a wild tempest, toward the middle of the opera, and, rising abruptly, he retired from the theatre. How still appeared the half deserted streets! Coldly the night air fell upon him, but the fever in his veins was unabated. He walked first up one street and then down another, with rapid steps, and this was continued for hours. Then the thought of going home crossed his mind. But he set his teeth firmly, and murmured audibly,

"Oh! to be defied, and charged with being a tyrant? And has it come to this so soon?"

The more Huntley brooded, in this unhappy mood, over his wife's words and conduct, the denser and more widely refracting became the medium through which he saw. His pride continually excited his mind, and threw a thick veil over all the gentler emotions of his heart. He was beside himself.

At one o'clock he found himself standing in front of the United States Hotel, his mind made up to desert the affectionate young creature, who, in a moment of thoughtlessness, had set her will in opposition to his,—to leave the city, under an assumed name, by the earliest lines, and go, he knew not nor cared not where. Blind passion was his prompter and guide. In this feverish state he entered the hotel and called for a bed.

Eleven, twelve, one o'clock came, and found Mrs. Huntley in a state of wild agitation. Edward had not yet returned. The silence and evident distress of Mrs. Carlisle struck down the heart of Esther, almost as much as her own fears. The too vivid recollection of one terrible event in her own life completely unbalanced the aunt's mind, and took away all power to sustain her niece.

"I will go in search of him, aunt!" exclaimed Esther, as the clock struck two. "He cannot leave the city before daylight. I will find him, and confess all my folly before it is too late."

"But where will you go, my child?" Mrs. Carlisle asked in a sad voice.

"Where—where shall I go?" eagerly inquired Mrs. Huntley.

"It is midnight, Esther. You cannot find him now."

"But I must see him before he leaves me, perhaps for ever! It will kill me. If I wait until morning, it will be too late."

Mrs. Carlisle bent her eyes to the floor, and for the space of more than a minute remained in deep thought. She then said, in a calm voice,

"Esther, I cannot believe that Edward will desert you on so slight a provocation. For a few hours his mind may be blinded with passion, and be swayed by false judgment. But morning will find him cooler and more reflective. He will see his error, and repent of any mad act he may have contemplated. Still, to guard against the worst of consequences, should this salutary change not take place, I think it would be best for you to go early to the boat, and by meeting him prevent a step that may cost you each a life of wretchedness."

"I will do it! He shall not go away! Oh! if I could once more meet him! all would be reconciled on the instant."

Confident in her own mind that Edward had determined to go away from the city in the morning, and fully resolved upon what she would do, Esther threw herself upon the bed, and in snatches of uneasy slumber passed the remainder of that dreadful night. At day-dawn she was up, and making preparations for going to the boat to intercept her husband.

"Be self-possessed, my dear niece," urged Mrs. Carlisle, in a voice that trembled so she could scarcely speak.

Esther tried to reply, but, though her lips and tongue moved, there was no utterance. Turning away, just as the sun threw his first rays into her chamber window, she went down stairs, and her aunt, no longer able to restrain herself, covered her face with her hands and wept.

On the day before, Esther had laid her gloves on one of the parlour mantels, and she went in to get them. It was so dark that she could not see, and she, therefore, opened a window and pushed back one of the shutters. As she did so, a sound between a sigh and a groan fell upon her ear, and caused her to turn with a start. There lay her husband, asleep upon one of the sofas! A wild cry that she could not restrain burst from her lips, and, springing toward him, she threw her arms about his neck as he arose, startled, from his recumbent position.

An hour's reflection, alone in the room he had taken at the hotel, satisfied Huntley that he was wrong in not going home. By the aid of his night key he entered, silently, at the very time his wife resolved to seek him in the morning, and, throwing himself upon a sofa in the parlour to think what he should next do, thought himself to sleep.

All was, of course, reconciled. With tears of joy and contrition Esther acknowledged the error she had committed. Huntley had his own share of blame in his impatient temper, and this he was also ready to confess He did not, however, own that he had thought of deserting his wife on such slight provocation, nor did she confess the fearful suspicion that had crossed her mind.

It was their first and last quarrel.

GUESS WHO IT IS!

"IT will be great deal better for us, Lizzy. America is a country where all things are in full and plenty; but here we are ground down to the earth and half-starved by the rich and great in order that they may become richer and greater. I isn't so there, Lizzy. Don't you remember what John McClure wrote home, six months after he crossed the ocean?"

"Yes, I remember all that, Thomas; but John McClure was never a very truthful body at home and I've always thought that if we knew every thing, we would find that he wrote with his magnifying glasses on. John, you know, was very apt to see things through magnifying glasses."

"But the testimony doesn't come alone from John. We hear it every day and from every quarter, that America is a perfect paradise for the poor, compared to England."

"I don't know how that can be, Thomas. They say that it is full of wild beast poisonous serpents, and savage Indians, and that the people are in constant fear of their lives. I'm sure England is a better place than that, even if we do have to work hard and get but little for it."

"All that used to be, Lizzy," replied Thomas. "But they've killed the wild beasts and serpents, and tamed the savage Indians. And there are great cities there, the same as in England."

But Lizzy could not be convinced. From her earliest childhood she had never had but one idea of America, and that was as a great wilderness filled with Indians and wild beasts. Of the former, she had heard tales that made her blood curdle in her veins. It was in vain, therefore, for Thomas Ward to argue with his wife about going to America. She was not to be convinced that a waste, howling wilderness was at all comparable with happy old England, even if the poor were "ground down."

As a dozen previous discussions on the subject had ended, so ended this. Thomas Ward was of the same mind as before, and so was his wife. The one wished to go, and the other to stay.

Ward had only been married a short time, but the period, short as it was, proved long enough to bring a sad disappointment of his worldly hopes. He had been employed as a gentleman's gardener for many years, and had been able, by strict economy, to lay up a little money. But soon after his, marriage, through some slight misunderstanding he lost his place, and had not since been able to obtain any thing more than transient employment, the return from which had, so far, proved inadequate to the maintenance of himself and wife, requiring him to draw steadily upon the not very large fund that was deposited in the Savings' Bank.

About once a fortnight Thomas would become completely discouraged, and then he invariably introduced his favourite project of going to America; but Lizzy always met him when in this mood with a decided negative, as far as she was concerned and sometimes went so far as to say, when he grew rather warm on the subject—"It's no use to talk about it, Thomas; I shall never go to America, that's decided."

This, instead of being a settler, as Lizzy supposed it would be, only proved a silencer. Thomas would instantly waive all present reference to the subject. But the less he talked, the more he thought about the land of plenty beyond the ocean; and the oftener Lizzy said she would never go to America, the more earnest became his desire to go, and the more fully formed his resolution to emigrate while possessed the ability to do so. He did not like Lizzy's mode of silencing him when he talked about his favourite theme. He had certain primitive notions about a wife's submission of herself to her husband, and it not only fretted him, but made him a little resolute on the subject of going to America when Lizzy declared herself determined not to go.

One day Ward came home with brows knit more closely than usual, and a firmer and more decided expression upon his tightly-closed lips.

"What's the matter now, Thomas?" asked his wife.

The "now" indicated that Thomas had something to trouble him, more or less, nearly all the time.

"The matter is, that I'm going to America!" returned Ward, in an angry tone of voice. "If you won't wish to go, you will only have to stay where you are. But I've made up my mind to sail in the next ship."

Ward had never spoken to his young wife in such harsh, angry, rebuking tone of voice since they were married. But the import of what he said was worse than his manner of saying it. Going to America—and going whether she chose to go with him or remain behind! What was this less than desertion? But Lizzy had pride and firmness as tell as acute sensibilities. The latter she controlled by means of the former, and, with unexpected coolness, replied—"Well, Thomas, if you wish to leave me, I have nothing to say. As to that savage country, I say now only what I have said before—I cannot go."

"Very well; I am not going to stay here and starve."

"We haven't starved yet, Thomas," spoke up Lizzy.

"No, thanks to my prudence in saving every dollar I could spare while a bachelor! But we're in a fair way for it now. Every week we are going behindhand, and if we stay here much longer we shall neither have the means of living nor getting away. I've finished my job, and cannot get another stroke to do."

"Something will turn up, Thomas; don't be impatient."

"Impatient!" ejaculated Ward.

"Yes, impatient, Thomas," coolly said his wife. "You are in a very strange way. Only wait a little while, and all will come right."

"Lizzy," said Thomas Ward, suddenly growing calm, and speaking slowly and with marked emphasis—"I've decided upon going to America. If you will go with me, as a loving and obedient wife should, I shall be glad of your company; but if you prefer to remain here, I shall lay no commands upon you. Will you or will you not go? Say at a word."

Lizzy had a spice of independence about her, as well as a good share of pride. The word "obedience," as applied to a wife, had never accorded much with her taste, and the use of it made on the present occasion by her husband was particularly offensive to her. So she replied, without pausing to reflect—"I have already told you that I am not going to America."

"Very well, Lizzy," replied Thomas, in a voice that was considerably softened, "I leave you to your own choice, notwithstanding the vow you made on that happy morning. My promise was to love you and to keep you in sickness and in health, but though I may love you as well in old England as in a far-off country, I cannot perform that other promise so well. So I must e'en leave you with my heart's best blessing, and a pledge that you shall want for no earthly comfort while I have a hand to work."

And saying this, Thomas Ward left the presence of his wife, and started forth to walk and to think. On his return, he found Lizzy sitting by the window with her hands covering her face, and the tears making their way through her fingers. He said nothing, but he had a hope that she would change her mind and go with him when the time came. In a little while Lizzy was able to control herself, and move silently about her domestic duties; but her husband looked into her face for some sign of a relenting purpose, and looked in vain.

On the next day, Ward said to his wife—"I've engaged my passage in the Shamrock, that sails from Liverpool for New York in a week."

Lizzy started, and a slight shiver ran through; her body; but a cold "Very well" was the only reply she made.

"I will leave twenty pounds in the Savings' Bank for you to draw out as you need. Before that is gone, I hope to be able to send you more money."

Lizzy made no answer to this, nor did she display any feeling, although, as she afterwards owned, she felt as if she would have sunk through the floor, and sorely repented having said that she would not go with her husband to America.

The week that intervened between that time and the sailing of the Shamrock passed swiftly away. Lizzy wished a hundred times that her husband would refer to his intended voyage across the sea, and ask her again if she would not go with him. But Thomas Ward had no more to say upon the subject. At least as often as three times had his wife refused to accompany him to a land where there was plenty of work and good wages, and he was firm in his resolution not to ask her again.

As the time approached nearer and nearer, Lizzy's heart sank lower and lower in her bosom; still she cherished all possible justifying reasons for her conduct, and sometimes had bitter thoughts against her husband. She called him, in her mind, arbitrary and tyrannical, and charged him with wishing to make her the mere slave of his will. As for Ward he also indulged in mental criminations, and tried his best to believe that Lizzy had no true affection for him, that she was selfish, self-willed, and the dear knows what all.

Thus stood affairs when the day came upon which the Shamrock was to sail, and Ward must leave in the early train of cars for Liverpool, to be on board at the hour of starting. Lizzy had done little but cry all night, and Thomas had lain awake thinking of the unnatural separation, and listening to his wife's but half-stifled sobs that ever and anon broke the deep silence of their chamber. At last daylight came, and Ward left his sleepless pillow to make hurried preparations for his departure. His wife arose also, and got ready his breakfast. The hour of separation at length came.

"Lizzy," said the unhappy but firm-hearted man, "we must now part. Whether we shall ever meet again, Heaven only knows. I do not wish to blame you in this trying moment, in this hour of grief to both, but I must say that—No, no!" suddenly checking himself, "I will say nothing that may seem unkind. Farewell! If ever your love for your husband should become strong enough to make you willing to share his lot in a far-off and stranger land, his arms and heart will be open to receive you."

Ward was holding the hand of his wife and looking into her face, over which tears, in spite of all her efforts to control herself, were falling. The impulse in Lizzy's heart was to throw herself into her husband's arms; but, as that would have been equivalent to giving up, and saying—"I must go with you, go where you will," she braved it out up to the last moment, and stood the final separation without trusting her voice in the utterance of a single word.

"God bless you, Lizzy!" were the parting words of the unhappy emigrant, as he wrung the passive hand of his wife, and then forced himself away.

The voyage to New York was performed in five weeks. On his arrival in that city, Ward sought among his countrymen for such information as would be useful to him in obtaining employment. By some of these, the propriety of advertising was suggested. Ward followed the suggestion, and by so doing happily obtained, within a week after his arrival, the offer of a good situation as overseer and gardener upon a large farm fifty miles from the city. The wages were far better than any he had received in England.

"Are you a single man?" asked the sturdy old farmer, after Ward had been a day or two at his new home.

"No, sir; I have a wife in the old country," he replied, with a slight appearance of confusion.

"Have you? Well, Thomas, why didn't you bring her along?"

"She was not willing to come to this country," returned Thomas.

"Then why did you come?"

"Because it was better to do so than to starve where I was."

"It doesn't matter about your wife, I suppose?"

"Why not?" Thomas spoke quickly, and knit his brows.

"If *you* couldn't live in England, what is your *wife* to do?"

"I shall send her half of my wages."

"Ah, that's the calculation, is it? But it seems to me that it would have been a saving in money as well as comfort, if she had come with you. Does she know any thing about dairy work?"

"Yes, sir; she was raised on a dairy farm."

"Then she's a regular-bred English dairy maid?"

"She is, and none better in the world."

"Just the person I want. You must write home for her, Thomas, and tell her she must come over immediately."

But Thomas shook his head.

"Won't she come?"

"I cannot tell. But she refused to come with me, although I repeatedly urged her. She must now take her own course. I felt, it to be my duty to her as well as to myself, to leave England for a better land; and if she thinks it her duty to stay behind, I must bear the separation the best way I can."

"I hope you had no quarrel, Thomas?" said the farmer, in his blunt way.

"No, sir," said Thomas, a little indignantly. "We never had the slightest difference, except in this matter."

"Then write home by the next steamer and ask her to join you, and she will be here by the earliest packet, and glad to come."

But Thomas shook his head. The man had his share of stubborn pride.

"As you will," said the farmer. "But I can tell you what, if she'd been my wife, I'd have taken her under my arm and brought her along in spite of all objections. It's too silly, this giving up to and being fretted about a woman's whims and prejudices. I'll be bound, if you'd told her she must come, and packed her trunk for her to show that you were in earnest, she'd never have dreamed of staying behind."

That evening Thomas wrote home to his wife all about the excellent place he had obtained, and was particular to say that he had agreed to remain for a year, and would send her half of his wages every month. Not one word, however, did he mention of the conversation that had passed between him and the farmer; nor did he hint, even remotely, to her joining him in the United States.

All the next day Thomas thought about what the farmer had said, and thought how happy both he and Lizzy might be if she would only come over and take charge of the dairy. The longer this idea remained present in his mind, the more deeply did it fix itself there. On the second night he dreamed that Lizzy was with him, that she had come over in the very next packet, and that they were as happy as they could be. He felt very bad when he awoke and found that it was only a dream.

At last, after a week had passed, Thomas Ward fully forgave his wife every thing, and sat himself down to write her a long letter, filled with all kinds of arguments, reasons, and entreaties favourable to a voyage across the Atlantic. Thus he wrote, in part:—

......."As to wild Indians, Lizzy, of which you have such fear, there are none within a thousand miles, and they are tame enough. The fierce animals are all killed, and I have not seen a single serpent, except a garter snake, that is as harmless as a tow string. Come then, Lizzy, come! I have not known a happy moment since I left you, and I am sure you cannot be happy. This is a land of peace and plenty—a land where—"

Thomas Ward did not know that a stranger had entered the room, and was now looking over his shoulder, and reading what he had written. Just as his pen was on the sentence left unfinished above, a pair of soft hands were suddenly drawn across his eyes, and a strangely familiar voice said, tremblingly—"Guess who it is!"

Before he had time to think or to guess, the hands passed from his eyes to his neck, and a warm wet cheek was laid tightly against his own. He could not see the face that lay so close to his, but he knew that Lizzy's arms were around him, that her tears were upon his face, and that her heart was beating against him.

"Bless us!" ejaculated the old farmer, who had followed after the young woman who had asked at the door with such an eager interest for Thomas Ward—"what does all this mean?"

By this time Thomas had gained a full view of his wife's tearful but happy face. Then he hugged her to his bosom over and over again, much to the surprise and delight of the farmer's urchins, who happened to be in the room.

"Here she is, sir; here she is!" he cried to the farmer, as soon as he could see any thing else but Lizzy's face, and then first became aware of the old gentleman's presence; "here is your English dairy maid."

"Then it's your wife, Thomas, sure enough."

"Oh, yes, sir; I thought she would be along after a while, but didn't expect this happiness so soon."

"How is this, my young lady?" asked the farmer, good-humouredly—"how is this? I thought you wasn't going to come to this country. But I suppose the very next packet after your husband left saw you on board. All I blame him for is not taking you under his arm, as I would have done, and bringing you along as so much baggage. But no doubt you found it much pleasanter coming over alone than it would have been in company with your husband—no doubt at all of it."

The kind-hearted farmer then took his children out of the room, and, closing the door, left the reunited husband and wife alone. Lizzy was too happy to say any thing about how wrong she had been in not consenting to go with her husband; but she owned that he had not been gone five minutes before she would have given the world, if she had possessed it, to have been with him. Ten days afterwards another packet sailed for the United States, and she took passage in it. On arriving in New York she was fortunate enough to fall in with a passenger who had come over in the Shamrock, and from him learned where she could find her husband, who acknowledged that she had given him the most agreeable surprise he had ever known in his life.

Lizzy has never yet had cause to repent of her voyage to America. The money she received for managing the dairy of the old farmer, added to what her husband could save from his salary, after accumulating for some years, was at length applied to the purchase of a farm, the produce of which, sold yearly in New York, leaves them a handsome annual surplus over and above their expenses. Thomas Ward is in a fair way of becoming a substantial and wealthy farmer.

MARRYING A TAILOR.

"KATE, Kate!" said Aunt Prudence, shaking her head and finger at the giddy girl.

"It's true, aunt. What! marry a tailor? The ninth part of a man, that doubles itself down upon a board, with thimble, scissors, and goose! Gracious!"

"I've heard girls talk before now, Kate; and I've seen them act, too; and, if I am to judge from what I've seen, I should say that you were as likely to marry a tailor as anybody else."

"I'd hang myself first!"

"Would you?"

"Yes, or jump into the river. Do any thing, in fact, before I'd marry a tailor."

"Perhaps you would not object to a merchant tailor?"

"Perhaps I would, though! A tailor's a tailor, and that is all you can make of him. 'Merchant tailor!' Why not say merchant shoemaker, or merchant boot-black? Isn't it ridiculous?"

"Ah well, Kate," said Aunt Prudence, "you may be thankful if you get an honest, industrious, kind-hearted man for a husband, be he a tailor or a shoemaker. I've seen many a heart-broken wife in my day whose husband was not a tailor. It isn't in the calling, child, that you must look for honour or excellence, but in the man. As Burns says—'The man's the goud for a' that.'"

"But a *man* wouldn't stoop to be a tailor."

"You talk like a thoughtless, silly girl, as you are, Kate. But time will take all this nonsense out of you, or I am very much mistaken. I could tell you a story about marrying a tailor, that would surprise you a little."

"I should like, above all things in the world, to hear a story of any interest, in which a tailor was introduced."

"I think I could tell you one."

"Please do, aunt. It would be such a novelty. A very *rara avis.*, as brother Tom says. I shall laugh until my sides ache."

"If you don't cry, Kate, I shall wonder," said Aunt Prudence, looking grave.

"Cry? oh, dear! And all about a tailor! But tell the story, aunt."

"Some other time, dear."

"Oh, no. I'm just in the humour to hear it now. I'm as full of fun as I can stick, and shall need all this overflow of spirits to keep me up while listening to the pathetic story of a tailor."

"Perhaps you are right, Kate. It may require all the spirits you can muster," returned Aunt Prudence, in a voice that was quite serious. "So I will tell you the story now."

And Aunt Prudence thus began:

A good many years ago,—I was quite a young girl then,—two children were left orphans, at the age of eleven years. They were twins—brother and sister. Their names I will call Joseph and Agnes Fletcher. The death of their parents left them without friends or relatives; but a kind-hearted tailor and his wife, who lived neighbours, took pity on the children and gave them a home. Joseph was a smart, intelligent lad, and the tailor thought he could do no better by him than to teach him his trade. So he set him to work with the needle, occasionally sent him about on errands, and let him go to school during the slack season. Joseph was a willing boy, as well as attentive, industrious, and apt to learn. He applied himself to his books and also to his work, and thereby gave great satisfaction to the good tailor. Agnes was employed about the house by the tailor's wife, who treated her kindly.

As Joseph grew older, he became more useful to his master, for he rapidly acquired a knowledge of his trade, and did his work remarkably well. At the same time, a desire to improve his mind made him studious and thoughtful. While other boys were amusing themselves, Joseph was alone with his book. At the age of eighteen he had grown quite tall, and was manly in his appearance. He had already acquired a large amount of information on various subjects, and was accounted by those who knew him a very intelligent young man. About this time, a circumstance occurred that influenced his whole after-life. He had been introduced by a friend to several pleasant families, which he visited regularly. In one of these visits, he met a young lady, the daughter of a dry-goods dealer, toward whom he felt, from the beginning, a strong attachment. Her name was Mary Dielman. Led on by his feelings, he could not help showing her some attention, which she evidently received with satisfaction. One evening, he was sitting near where she was chatting away at a lively rate, in the midst of a gay circle of young girls, and, to his surprise, chagrin, and mortification, heard her ridiculing, as you too often do, the business at which he was serving an apprenticeship.

"Marry a tailor!" he heard her say, in a tone of contempt. "I would drown myself first."

This was enough. Joseph's feelings were like the leaves of a sensitive plant. He did not venture near the thoughtless girl during the evening, and whenever they again met, he was distant and formal. Still, the thought of her made the blood flow quicker through his veins, and the sight of her made his heart throb with a sudden bound.

From that time, Joseph, who had looked forward with pleasure to the period when, as a man, he could commence his business, and prosecute it with energy and success, became dissatisfied with the trade he was learning. The contemptuous words of Mary Dielman made him feel that there was something low in the calling of a tailor—something beneath the dignity of a man. He did not reason on the subject; he only felt. Gradually he withdrew himself from society, and shut himself up at home, devoting all his leisure to reading and study. This was continued until he attained the age of manhood, soon after which he procured the situation of clerk in a dry-goods store. At his trade he could easily earn twelve dollars a week; but he left it, because he was silly enough to be ashamed of it, and went into a dry-goods store at a salary of four hundred dollars a year. As a clerk he felt more like a man. Why he should, is more than I can comprehend. But so it was.

As for Mary Dielman, she was not aware, at the time when she felt so pleased with the attentions of Joseph Fletcher, that he was a tailor—a calling for which she always expressed the most supreme contempt. Her thoughtless words were not, therefore, meant for his ears. The fact that she had uttered them was not remembered ten minutes after they were spoken. Why she no longer met the fine-looking, attentive and intelligent young man, she did not know. Often she thought of him, and often searched the room for him, with her eyes, when in company.

Nearly four years passed before they again met. Then Joseph was greatly improved, and so was the beautiful maiden. The half-extinguished fire of love, that had been smouldering in their bosoms, rekindled, and now burned with a steady flame. They saw each other frequently, and it was not long before the young man told her all that was in his heart, and she heard the story with tremulous delight.

The father of Mary, although a merchant, was not nearly so well off in the world as many tailors. His family was expensive and drew too heavily upon his income. The capital employed in trade was therefore kept low, and his operations were often crippled for want of adequate means. He had nothing, therefore, to settle upon his daughter. When young Fletcher applied for her hand, his salary was five hundred dollars. Mr. Dielman thought his prospects not over flattering, but still gave his consent; at the same time advising him not to think of marriage for a year or two, when he would no doubt be in a better condition to take a wife.

The young couple, like most young couples, were impatient to be married; and Joseph Fletcher, in order to be in a condition that would justify him in talking a wife, was impatient to go into business. Somehow or other, it had entered his mind that any young man of business capacity and enterprise could do well in the West; and he finally made up his mind to take a stock of goods, which he found no difficulty in obtaining, and go to Madison, in Indiana. Before starting, however, he engaged to return in six months, or so soon as he was fairly under way, and make Mary his wife. At the time named, he was back, when the marriage took place, and he returned with his bride to Madison.

At the trade of a tailor, the young man had served an apprenticeship of seven years. He was a good workman, and had, during the last two years of his apprenticeship, assisted his master in cutting; so that in the art to which he was educated he was thoroughly at home; and, in setting it up, would have been sure of success. But success was by no means so certain a thing in the new pursuit unwisely adopted. He had been familiar with it for only about two years; in that time he had performed his part as a clerk to the entire satisfaction of his employers; but he had not gained sufficient knowledge of the principles of trade, nor was his experience enlarged enough to justify his entering into business, especially as he did not possess a dollar of real capital. The result was as might have been expected. A year and a half of great difficulty and anxiety was all the time required to bring his experiment to a close.

Finding that he was in difficulty, two or three of his principal eastern creditors, whose claims were due, sent out their accounts to a lawyer, With directions to put them in suit immediately. This brought his affairs to a crisis. An arrangement was made for the benefit of all the creditors, and the young man thrown out of business, with less than a hundred dollars in his pocket. Nearly about the same time, Mr. Dielman, the father of his wife, failed likewise.

As a serious loss has been sustained by his eastern creditors on account of the unfortunate termination of his business, Fletcher could not think of going back. He therefore sought to obtain employment as a clerk in Madison. Failing in this, he visited Louisville and Cincinnati, but with no better success. He was unknown in the two last-named cities, and therefore his failure to obtain employment there was no matter of surprise.

Things now wore a very serious aspect. A few weeks found the unhappy young man reduced to the extremity of breaking up and selling his furniture by auction in order to get money to live upon. There was scarcely a store in Madison at which he had not sought for employment. But all his efforts proved vain. He had a good trade; why, you will ask, did he not endeavour to get work at that? You forget. It was the trade of a tailor!—the calling so despised by his wife. How could he own to her that he was but a tailor! How could he break to her the disgraceful truth that she had married a tailor!

The money obtained by selling their furniture did not last a very long time.

"I will make another effort to obtain employment in Cincinnati," said the young man, after they were reduced almost to their last dollar. "It is useless to try any longer in this place. I have waited and hoped for some favourable turn of fortune, until my heart is sick."

His wife made no objection, for she had none to make.

On the next day, Fletcher left for Cincinnati. He arrived there in the night. On the following morning, he left the hotel at which he had stopped, and, going into Main street, entered the first merchant-tailor's shop that came in his way.

"Have you any work?" he asked.

"We have room for a journeyman, and are in want of one. Can you do the best work?"

"I can."

"Did you serve your time in the city?"

"No. I am from the East."

"Very well. Here is a job all ready. You can go to work at once."

The young man did not hesitate. He took the bundle of work that was given him, and was shown into the back shop. He wrote home immediately that he had obtained employment, which he hoped would be permanent, and that he would be in Madison, Saturday about midnight, and leave again on Sunday evening. He did not say, however, what kind of employment he had procured. That was a secret he meant, if possible, to conceal. When he met his wife, he evaded her direct questions as to the kind of employment he was engaged in, somewhat to her surprise.

For a month, Fletcher went and returned from Cincinnati, weekly, bringing home about eight dollars each week, after paying all his expenses. By that time, his wife insisted so strongly upon going to Cincinnati with him, and taking boarding, that he could make no reasonable objection to the step. And so they removed, Fletcher feeling many serious misgivings at heart, lest his wife should make a discovery of the truth that she had married only a tailor!

"Where did you say the store was at which you are employed?" she asked, a day or two after they were comfortably settled at a very pleasant boarding-house in Cincinnati.

"On Main street," replied Fletcher, a little coldly.

"What is the name of the firm? I forget."

"Carter & Cassard."

Fletcher could not lie outright to his wife, so he told her the truth, but with great reluctance.

No more was said then on the subject. About a week afterward, Mrs. Fletcher said to her husband, "I was along Main street to-day, and looked at the signs over every dry-goods store that I passed, but I did not see that of Carter & Cassard."

In spite of all he could do, the blood rushed to the face of the young man, and his eyes fell under the steady look directed toward him by his wife.

"The store is there, nevertheless," said he. His manner and the tone in which he spoke excited in the mind of his wife a feeling of surprise.

For the next four days, there was a strong conflict in Fletcher's mind between false pride and duty. It grieves me to say that, in the end, the former conquered. On Saturday night, he came home with a troubled look, and told his wife that he had lost his situation, which he said had only been a temporary one. In this he certainly went beyond the truth, for he had given it up voluntarily.

The poor young creature's heart sank in her. They had only been in Cincinnati about two weeks; were among entire strangers, and all means of subsistence were again taken from them. It is no wonder that she wept bitterly upon receiving this sudden and distressing intelligence. To see his wife in tears filled the heart of Fletcher with the severest pangs. He more than half repented of what he had done. But the thought of confessing that he was only a tailor made him firm in his resolution to meet any consequence rather than that.

"He was a fool!" exclaimed Kate, no longer able to restrain her indignation against the young man, and thus breaking in upon her aunt's narrative.

"But remember, Kate, how contemptuously he had heard her speak of his trade, and even vow that she would rather drown herself than marry a tailor."

"Suppose she did say this, when a thoughtless girl"—

"As you are, Kate."

"Don't bring me into the matter, aunt. But suppose she did say so, is that any reason for his starving her? He was bound to use his best efforts for the support of his family, and ought to have been thankful, under the circumstances, that he was a tailor."

"So I think. And his wife ought to have been thankful too."

"And I suppose she would have been if he had possessed the manliness to tell her the truth."

"No doubt in the world of that," returned Aunt Prudence, and then resumed her narrative:

A week was spent by the young man in another vain effort to find employment as a clerk. Then he avowed his intention to go to Louisville, and see if nothing could be done there.

"Try longer here, Joseph. Don't go away yet," earnestly and tearfully pleaded his wife. "You don't know how hard it is for me to be separated from you. I am lonely through the day, and the nights pass, oh! so heavily. Something may turn up for you here. Try for a while longer."

"But our money is nearly all gone. If I don't go now, I shall have no means of getting away from this place. I feel sure that I can find something to do there."

His wife pleaded with him, but in vain. To Louisville he went, and there got work at the first shop to which he made application. At the end of a week he sent his wife money, and told her that he had procured temporary employment. She wrote back asking if she might not join him immediately. But to this he objected, on the score that, as his situation was not a permanent one, he might, in a few weeks, be obliged to leave Louisville and go somewhere else. This, to his wife, was by no means satisfactory. But she could do no less than submit.

Thus separated, they lived for the next three months, Fletcher visiting his wife and child once every two weeks, and spending Sunday with them. During the time, he made good wages. But both himself and wife were very unhappy. Earnestly did the latter plead with her husband to be allowed to remove to Louisville. To this however, he steadily objected. Daily he lived in the hope of securing a clerkship in some store, and thus, being able to rise above the low condition in which he was placed. The moment he reached that consummation, so much desired, he would instantly remove his family.

At length, it happened that Fletcher did not write once, instead of several times, during one of the periods of two weeks that he was regularly absent. The Sunday morning when he was expected home arrived, but it did not bring, as usual, his anxiously looked-for presence. His wife was almost beside herself with alarm. No letter coming on Monday, she took her child and started for Louisville in the first boat. She arrived at daylight, on Tuesday morning, in a strange city, herself a total stranger to all therein, except her husband, and perfectly ignorant as to where he was to be found. The captain of the steamboat kindly attended her to a boarding-house, and there she was left, without a single clue in her mind as to the means of finding her husband. Inquiries were made of all in the boarding-house, but no one had heard even the name of Joseph Fletcher. As soon as she could make arrangements to get out, Mrs. Fletcher visited all the dry-goods stores in the city, for in some one of these she supposed her husband to be employed, although he had never stated particularly the kind of business in which he was engaged. This search, after being continued for a greater part of the day, turned out fruitless. Night found the unhappy wife in an agony of suspense and alarm. Some one at the boarding-house advised her to have an advertisement for her husband inserted in a morning paper. She did not hesitate long about this course. In the morning, a brief advertisement appeared; and about nine o'clock a man called and asked to see her.

She descended from her room to the parlour with a wildly throbbing heart, but staggered forward and sank into a chair, weak almost as an infant, when she saw that the man was a stranger, instead of her husband, whom she had expected to meet.

"Are you Mrs. Fletcher?" he asked.

"I am," she faintly replied.

"You advertised for information in regard to your husband?"

"I did. Where is he? Oh, sir, has any thing happened to him?"

"No, ma'am, nothing serious. He has only been sick for a week or ten days; that is, the man I refer to has. Your husband is a tailor?"

"Is the man you speak of a tailor?" eagerly asked Mrs. Fletcher.

"He is, ma'am; and has been working for me at No.—Fourth street."

"Then he is not my husband," replied the poor wife, bursting into tears. "My husband is a clerk." In the bitterness of a keen disappointment, rendered sharper by doubt and fear, Mrs. Fletcher wept for some minutes. When she could command her feelings to some extent, she thanked the tailor for calling, and repeated what she had said, that the man at his house could not be her husband.

"He is from Cincinnati, ma'am; and goes there once in every two weeks. I know that he has wife and child there," said the man.

"Still he cannot be my husband," replied Mrs. Fletcher; "for my husband is not a tailor."

"No, not in that case, certainly." And the man owed and withdrew.

All day long the wife waited for some more satisfactory reply to her advertisement, but no farther response to it was made. The call of the tailor seemed like a mockery of her unhappy condition.

Night came, and all remained in doubt and darkness; and then the mind of Mrs. Fletcher turned to the visit of the tailor, half despairingly, in order to find some feeble gleam of hope. Perhaps, she said to herself, as she thought about it, there is some mistake. Perhaps it is my husband after all, and the man is in some error about his being a tailor. As she thought, it suddenly flashed through her mind that there had been a good deal of mystery made by her husband about his situation in Cincinnati as well as in Louisville, which always struck her as a little strange. Could it be possible that his real business was that of a tailor? All at once she remembered that her husband had been particularly silent in regard to his early history. Trembling with excitement, she left the house about eight o'clock in the evening, and started for the place where she remembered that the tailor said he lived. He was in his shop, and recollected her the moment she entered.

"Can I see the man you told me was named Fletcher?" she asked.

"Yes, ma'am; and I sincerely hope there has been some mistake, and that you will find him to be your husband; for he is very ill, and needs to be nursed by a careful hand."

Mrs. Fletcher followed the tailor up stairs, her heart scarcely beating under the pressure of suspense. In a small chamber in the third story, the atmosphere of which was close, oppressive, and filled with an offensive odour, she was shown a man lying upon a bed. She needed not a second glance, as the dim light fell upon his pale, emaciated face, to decide her doubts. Her husband lay before her. Eagerly she called his name, but his eyes did not open. She spoke to him again and again, but he did not recognise, even if he heard her voice.

On inquiring, she found that he was ill with a violent fever, which the doctor said was about at its crisis. This had been brought on by too long continued labour—he having worked, often, sixteen and seventeen hours out of the twenty-four—by that means earning a third more wages than any journeyman in the shop.

Alarmed and troubled as she was, Mrs. Fletcher was utterly confounded by all this. She could not comprehend it. All night she hovered over the pillow of her husband, giving him medicine at the proper times, placing the cooling draught to his lips or bathing his hot forehead. Frequently she called his name, earnestly and tenderly, but the sound awoke no motions in his sluggish mind. Toward morning, she was sitting with her face resting against a pillow, when his voice, speaking distinctly, aroused her from a half slumber into which she had, momentarily, lost herself. In an instant she was leaning over him, with his name upon her lips. His eyes were opens and he looked steadily into her face. But it was evident that he did not know her.

"Joseph! Joseph! don't you know me?" said she. "I am your wife. I am here with you."

"Poor Mary!" he murmured, sadly, not understanding what was said. "If she knew all, it would break her heart."

"What would break her heart?" quickly asked his wife.

"Poor Mary! She said she would never marry"—here the sick man's voice became inarticulate.

But all was clear to the mind of Mrs. Fletcher. She remembered how often she had made the thoughtless remark to which her husband evidently referred. The tears again fell over her cheeks, until they dropped even upon the face of her husband, who, after he had said this, muttered for a while, inarticulately, and then, closing his eyes, went off into sleep.

Toward morning a slight moisture broke out all over him, and his sleep that was heavy, became soft and tranquil. The crisis was past! In order not to disturb the quiet slumberer, Mrs. Fletcher sat down by the bedside perfectly still. It was not very long before, over-wearied as she was, sleep likewise stole over her senses. It was daylight when she was awakened by hearing her name called. Starting up, she met the face of her husband turned earnestly toward her.

"Dear husband!" she exclaimed, "do you know me?"

"Yes, Mary. But how came you here?" he said, in a feeble voice.

"We will speak of that at some other time," she replied. "Enough that I am here, where I ought to have been ten days ago. But that was not my fault."

Fletcher was about to make some farther remark, when his wife placed her finger upon his lips, and said—

"You must not talk, dear; your disease has just made a favourable change, and your life depends upon your being perfectly quiet. Enough for me to say that I know all, and love you just as well, perhaps better. You are a weak, foolish man, Joseph," she added, with a smile, "or else thought me a weak and foolish woman. But all that we can settle hereafter. Thank God that I have found you; and that you are, to all appearances, out of danger."

Aunt Prudence looked into Kate's face, and saw that tears were on her cheeks.

"Would you have loved him less, Kate," she asked, "if he had been your husband?"

"He would have been the same to me whatever might have been his calling. That could not have changed him."

"No, certainly not. But I have a word or two more to add. As soon as Fletcher was well enough to go to work, he took his place again upon the shop-board, his wife feeling happier than she had felt for a long time. In about six months he rose to be foreman of the shop, and a year after that became a partner in the business At the end of ten years he sold out his interest in the business, and returned to the East with thirty thousand dollars in cash. This handsome capital enabled him to get into an old and well-established mercantile house as partner, where he remained until his death. About the time of his return to the East, you, Kate, were born."

"I!" ejaculated the astonished girl.

"Yes. Their two older children died while they were in Louisville, and you, their third child, were born about six months before they left."

"I!" repeat Kate, in the same surprised tone of voice.

"Yes, dear, you! I have given you a history of your own father and mother. So, as you're the daughter of a tailor, you must not object to a tailor for a husband, if he be the right kind of a man."

It may very naturally be supposed that Kate had but little to say against tailors after that, although we are by no means sure that she had any intention of becoming the bride of one.

THE MAIDEN'S CHOICE.

"TWO offers at once! You are truly a favoured maiden, Rose," said Annette Lewis to her young friend Rose Lilton, in a gay tone. "It is husband or no husband with most of us; but you have a choice between two."

"And happy shall I be if I have the wisdom to choose rightly," was the reply of Rose.

"If it were my case, I don't think that I should have much difficulty in making a choice."

"Don't you? Suppose, then, you give me the benefit of your preference."

"Oh, no, not for the world!" replied Annette, laughing. "I'm afraid you might be jealous of me afterwards."

"Never fear. I am not of a jealous disposition."

"No, I won't commit myself in regard to your lovers. But, if they were mine, I would soon let it be known where my preference lay."

"Then you won't assist me in coming to a decision? Surely I am entitled to this act of friendship."

"If you put it upon that ground, Rose, I do not see how I can refuse."

"I do put it upon that ground, Annette. And now I ask you, as a friend, to give me your opinion of the two young men, James Hambleton and Marcus Gray, who have seen such wonderful attractions in my humble self as to become suitors for my hand at the same time."

"Decidedly, then, Rose, I should prefer Marcus Gray."

"There is about him, certainly, Annette, much to attract a maiden's eye and to captivate her heart but it has occurred to me that the most glittering surface does not always indicate the purest gold beneath. I remember once to have seen a massive chain, wrought from pure ounces, placed beside another that was far inferior in quality, but with a surface of ten times richer hue. Had I not been told the difference, I would have chosen the latter as in every way more valuable; but when it was explained that one bore the hue of genuine gold, while the other had been coloured by a process known to jewellers, I was struck with the lesson it taught."

"What lesson, Rose?"

"That the richest substance has not always the most glittering exterior. That real worth, satisfied with the consciousness of interior soundness of principle, assumes few imposing exterior aspects and forms."

"And that rule you apply to these two young men?"

"By that rule I wish to be guided, in some degree, in my choice, Annette. I wish to keep my mind so balanced, that it may not be swayed from a sound discrimination by any thing of imposing exterior."

"But is not the exterior—that which meets the eye—all that we can judge from? Is not the exterior a true expression of what is within?"

"Not by any means, Annette. I grant that it should be, but it is not. Look at the fact I have just named respecting the gold chains."

"But they were inanimate substances. They were not faces, where thoughts, feelings, and principles find expression."

"Do you suppose, Annette, that bad gold would ever have been coloured so as to look even more beautiful than that which is genuine, if there had not been men who assumed exterior graces and virtues that were not in their minds? No. The very fact you adduce strengthens my position. The time was, in the earlier and purer ages—the golden ages of the world's existence —when the countenance was the true index to the mind. Then it was a well-tuned instrument, and the mind within a skilful player; to whose touch every muscle, and chord, and minute fibre gave answering melody. That time has passed. Men now school their faces to deception; it is an art which nearly all practise—I and you too often. We study to hide our real feelings; to appear, in a certain sense, what we are not. Look at some men whom we meet every day, with faces whose calmness, I should rather say rigidity, gives no evidence that a single emotion ever crosses the waveless ocean of their minds. But it is not so; the mind within is active with thought and feelings; but the instrument formed for it to play upon has lost its tune, or bears only relaxed or broken chords."

"You have a strange, visionary way of talking sometimes, Rose," replied Annette, as her friend ceased speaking. "All that may do for your transcendentalists, or whatever you call them; but it won't do when you come down to the practical matter-of-fact business of life."

"To me, it seems eminently a practical principle, Annette. We must act, in all important matters in life, with a just discrimination; and how can we truly discriminate, if we are not versed in those principles upon which, and only upon which, right discriminations can be made?"

"I must confess, Rose," replied her young friend, "that I do not see much bearing that all this has upon the matter under discussion; or, at least, I cannot see the truth of its application. Gold never assumes a leaden exterior."

"Well?"

"We need not be very eminent philosophers to tell one from the other."

"No, of course not."

"Very well. Here is Marcus Gray, with a genuine golden exterior, and James Hambleton with a leaden one."

"I do not grant the position, Annette. It is true that Mr. Hambleton is not so brilliant and showy; but I have found in him one quality that I have not yet discovered in the other."

"What is that?"

"Depth of feeling, and high moral principle."

"You certainly do not pretend to affirm that Mr. Gray has neither feeling nor principle?"

"Of course I do not. I only say that I have never yet perceived any very strong indications of their existence."

"Why, Rose!"

"I am in earnest, Annette. I doubt not that he possesses both, and, I trust, in a high degree. But he seems to be so constantly acting a brilliant and effective part, that nature, unadorned and simple, has no chance to speak out. It is not so with Mr. Hambleton. Every word he utters shows that he is speaking what he really feels; and often, though not so highly polished in speech as Mr. Gray, have I heard him utter sentiments of genuine truth and humanity, in a tone that made my heart bound with pleasure at recognising the simple eloquence of nature. His character, Annette, I find it no way difficult to read; that of Marcus Gray puzzles my closest scrutiny."

"I certainly cannot sympathize with you in your singular notions, Rose," her friend replied. "I have never discovered either of the peculiarities in these young men that you seem to make of so much importance. As for Mr. Gray, he is a man of whom any woman might feel proud; for he combines intelligence with courteous manners and a fine person: while this Hambleton is, to me, insufferably stupid. And no one, I am sure, can call his address and manners any thing like polished. Indeed, I should pronounce him downright boorish and awkward. Who would want a man for a husband of whom she would be ashamed? Not I, certainly."

"I will readily grant you, Annette," said Rose, as her friend ceased speaking, "that Mr. Hambleton's exterior attractions are not to be compared with those of Mr. Gray; but, as I said before, in a matter like this, where it is the quality of the mind, and not the external appearance of the man alone, that is to give happiness, it behooves a maiden to look beneath the surface, as I am trying to do now."

"But I could not love a man like Mr. Hambleton, unless, indeed, there were no possibility of getting any one else. In that case, I would make a choice of evils between single blessedness and such a husband. But to have two such offers as these, Rose, and hesitate to make a choice, strikes me as singular indeed!"

"I do not hesitate, Annette," was the quiet reply.

"Have you, then, indeed decided, Rose?"

"I have—and this conversation has caused me to decide; for, as it has progressed, my mind has been enabled to see truly the real difference in the characters of my suitors."

"You have, then, decided in favor of Mr. Gray?"

"Indeed I have not, Annette. Though I admire his fine talents and his polished exterior, yet I have never been able to perceive in him those qualities upon which my heart can rest in confidence. He may possess these in even a higher degree than Mr. Hambleton, but I am afraid to run so great a risk. In the latter, I know there are moral qualities that I can love, and that I can repose upon."

"But he is so dull, Rose."

"I really do not think so, Annette. There is not so much flash about him, if I may use the word, as about Mr. Gray. But as to his being dull, I must beg to differ with you. To me, his conversation is always interesting."

"It never is so to me. And, besides all that, his tastes and mine are as widely different as the poles. Why, Rose, if you become his wife, you will sink into obscurity at once. He never can make any impression on society. It is not in him."

"Rather make no impression on society at all, than a false or disgraceful one, say I," was the firm reply of Rose.

"You cannot, certainly, mean to say," returned her friend, "that the impression made upon society by Mr. Gray is either a false or disgraceful one."

"I should be sorry to make that assertion, for I do not believe such to be the case," Rose replied. "What I mean is, that I can read Mr. Hambleton's true character, and I know it to be based upon fixed and high-toned principles. These can never make the woman who truly loves him unhappy. They give place to no moral contingencies, by which hopes are so often wrecked, and hearts broken. Now, in regard to Mr. Gray, there is nothing in his character, so far as I can, read it, upon which to predicate safe calculations of this kind. He is intelligent, and highly interesting as a companion. His personal appearance and his address are attractive. But all below the exterior is hidden. The moral qualities of the man never show themselves. I feel that to give my heart to such a one would be risking too much. Of course, I must decline his offer."

"Indeed, indeed, Rose, I think you are very foolish!"

"Time will show, Annette."

"Yes, time will show," was the prophetic response. And time did show that Rose made a right choice, when she accepted the offer of James Hambleton, and gave him, with her hand, a warm, true heart.

THE FORTUNE-HUNTER.

"I KNOW a young lady who will suit you exactly."

"Indeed!"

"It's a fact. She is just the thing."

"Is she rich?"

"Of course."

"How rich?"

"Worth some fifty thousand dollars."

"Are you sure?"

"Certainly. Her father died about a year ago, and she was his only child. Her mother has been dead many years. The old man was well off, and his daughter received all of his property, and, as she is of age, she has it all under her own control."

"Is she handsome?"

"Just so-so. But that don't matter a great deal. Gold is beautiful."

"Exactly. And intelligent?"

"I've seen smarter girls. But that's all the better, you know."

"Yes. Well now, who is she? That's the next question."

"Her name is Margaretta Riston, and she is now living with an old aunt in Sycamore street."

"Are you acquainted?"

"Intimately."

"Then be kind enough to introduce me forthwith. I must make a conquest of some rich heiress soon, or I shall have to run away, or petition for the benefit of the Insolvent Law."

"To-night, if you choose."

"Very well—let it be to-night. There is no time to be lost."

"Suppose she won't accept you?"

"She must. I'm as good-looking a fellow as you'll find in a dozen; and I flatter myself that I have a smooth tongue in my head."

"Well, success to you, I say! But look here, Smith: if you succeed, I shall expect a premium."

"There'll be no difficulty about that, Perkins. But let me secure the prize first; and then say how much you'll want. You'll not find me the man to forget a friend."

"I'm sure of that," responded the other, laughing.

And then the friends shook each other's hands heartily, promising, as they parted, to meet early in the evening, preparatory to visiting the heiress.

"You would not have me suspicious of every young man who visits me!" said Margaretta Riston, in reply to a remark made by her aunt, on the same evening that the two young men had proposed calling on her.

"I would rather have you suspicious, or, rather, exceedingly watchful, than to be altogether off of your guard. Many dangers beset the path of a rich young girl like you. There are, and I am sorry to say it, too many young men in society, who are mere money-hunters—young men who would marry an heiress during the first hour of their acquaintance, and marry her, of course, only for her money."

"I can hardly credit it, aunt. And I am sure that no young men of my acquaintance are so selfish and mercenary!"

"In that assumption lies a fatal error, believe me, my dear niece! Too many, alas! too many young girls have vainly imagined, as you do now, that, though there might be men of base characters in society, none such were of their acquaintances. These have awakened from their fatal error with the sad consciousness that they had become victims to their fond infidelity. Rather suspect all until you have convincing evidence to the contrary, than remain unguarded until it is too late."

"But don't you see, aunt, how in this case I would do wrong to sincere and honest minds? And I cannot bear the thought of doing wrong to any one."

"You do no wrong to any one, my niece, in with-holding full confidence until there is evidence that full confidence may be safely bestowed. In the present evil state of the world, involving, as it does, so much of false appearance, hypocrisy, and selfish motive, it is absolutely necessary, especially with one in your situation, to withhold all confidence, until there is unquestionable proof of virtuous principle."

"There is at least one young man, who visits here, that I think is above such mean suspicions," Margaretta said.

"So I think," the aunt replied.

"Whom do you mean, aunt?"

"I mean Thomas Fielding."

"Thomas Fielding! Well, he may be; but—"

"But what, Margaretta?"

"Oh, nothing, aunt. But I do not like Mr. Fielding so very much."

"Why not, child?"

"I can hardly tell. But there is no character about him."

"No character! Really, Margaretta, you surprise me. There is more character and principle about him than about any young man who comes to this house."

"I cannot think so, aunt. He is too tame, prosy, and old-fashioned for me."

"Whom then did you mean?" the aunt asked, with an expression of concern in her tones.

"Why, Mr. Perkins, to be sure."

The aunt shook her head.

"I am afraid, Margaretta, that Mr. Perkins is a man of few principles, but thoroughly selfish ones."

"How strangely you talk, aunt! Why, he is any thing but a selfish man. I am sure he is the most gentlemanly, thoughtful, and polite man that visits here. He is much more attentive to others, in company, than Mr. Fielding; and that, I am sure, indicates a kinder regard for others."

"Not always, Margaretta. It may sometimes indicate a cold-hearted, calm assurance, assumed for selfish ends; while its opposite may be from a natural reserve or timidity of character."

"But you don't mean to say, surely, that Mr. Perkins is such a one as you intimate?"

"If I am correct in my observation, he is all that I have insinuated. In a word, he is, in my opinion, a mere money-hunter."

"I am sure, aunt, he is not so constant in his attentions as he was some time, ago; and, if he were merely a money-hunter, he would not, of course, abate those attentions."

"No—not unless he had discovered a richer prize."

"Indeed, aunt, you wrong him."

"I should be sorry to do so, Margaretta. But I do not form my opinions hastily. I try to look close before I come to conclusions. But I have stronger testimony than my own observations."

"What is that?"

"Why, I heard this morning that he is to be married in a few weeks to Harriet Pomeroy."

"Indeed, you must be mistaken, aunt," said Margaretta, suddenly rising to her feet.

"I presume not," was the quiet reply. "My information came almost direct."

The entrance of visitors now interrupted the conversation.

"Permit me to introduce my very particular friend, Mr. Smith," said the individual about whom the aunt and her niece were conversing, as he entered the handsome parlour of Mrs. Riston.

Mr. Smith and Mr. Perkins were, of course, received with great affability by Margaretta, who concealed the impression made upon her mind by the piece of information just conveyed by her aunt.

As for Mrs. Riston, she was studiedly polite, but gave the young men no very apparent encouragement. An hour soon passed away, and then the visitors retired.

"Well, Smith, what do you think of her?" asked Perkins, as the two gained the street.

"You're sure she's worth fifty thousand dollars?"

"Oh, yes. There's no mistake about that."

"But *how* do you know? This is a matter about which there should be no mistake."

"I got a friend to examine the transfer books of the bank where the stock is. Will that satisfy you?"

"You did? And pray why did you do that?"

"A strange question! but I'll tell you, as you seem dull. I had a notion of her myself."

"You had?"

"I had."

"And why did you get out of the notion?"

"Because I saw another whom I liked better."

"She was richer, I suppose."

"How can you insinuate such a thing?" And Perkins laughed in a low, meaning chuckle.

"Ah, I perceive. Well, how much is she worth?"

"About a hundred thousand."

"Are you sure of her?"

"Certainly! The thing's all settled."

"You're a lucky dog, Perkins! But see here, what did you mean by the premium you talked of for bringing about a match between me and Miss Riston?"

"Oh, as to that, I was only jesting. But you haven't told me how you like the young lady yet."

"Oh, she'll do, I reckon," said Smith, tossing his head half contemptuously.

"Do you think you can secure her?"

"Easily enough. But then I must get her away as often as possible from that old Cerberus of an aunt. I didn't like her looks at all."

"She's suspicious."

"That's clear. Well, she must be wide awake if I commence playing against her in real earnest. I can win any girl's affections that I choose."

"You have a pretty fair conceit of yourself, I see."

"I wouldn't give a cent for a man that hadn't. The fact is, Perkins, these girls have but one end in view, and that is to get married. They know that they have to wait to be asked, and, trembling in fear lest they shall not get another offer, they are always ready to jump eagerly at the first."

"Pretty true, I believe. But, Smith, don't you think Margaretta quite a fair specimen of a girl?"

"Oh, yes. And I have no doubt that I shall love her well enough, if she don't attempt to put on airs, and throw up to me that she was rich, and I poor. I'll never stand that."

"She'll not be so foolish, I presume."

"She'd better not, I can tell her, if she doesn't wish to get into hot water." And the young man laughed at his own half-in-earnest jesting.

"He's a very agreeable young man, isn't he, aunt?" said Margaretta, after the two young men had gone away.

"Who? Mr. Smith, as Mr. Perkins called him?"

"Yes."

"He has a smooth enough tongue, if that is any recommendation; but I do not like him. Indeed, he is far more disagreeable to me than his very particular friend, Mr. Perkins."

"Oh, aunt, how can you talk so! I'm sure he was very agreeable. At least, I thought so."

"That was because he flattered you so cleverly."

"How *can* you insinuate such a thing, aunt? Surely I am not so weak and vain as to be imposed upon and beguiled by a flatterer!"

"Some men understand how to flatter very ingeniously; and, to me, Mr. Smith seemed peculiarly adept in the art. He managed it so adroitly as to give it all the effect, without its being apparent to the subject of his experiments."

"Indeed, aunt, you are mistaken. I despise a flatterer as much as you do. But I am sure that I saw nothing like flattery about Mr. Smith."

"I am sorry that you did not, Margaretta. But take my advice, and be on your guard. That man's motives in coming to see you, believe me, are not the purest in the world."

"You are far too suspicious, aunt; I am sure you are."

"Perhaps I have had cause. At any rate, Margaretta, I have lived longer in, and seen much more of the world than you have, and I ought to have a clearer perception of character. For your own sake, then, try and confide in my judgment."

"I ought to confide in your judgment, aunt, I know; but I cannot see as you do in this particular instance."

"Then you ought rather to suspect the correctness of your own observation, when it leads to conclusions so utterly opposed to mine."

To this Margaretta did not reply. It seemed too much like giving up her own rationality to assent to it, and she did not wish to pain her aunt by objections.

On the next evening, a quiet, intelligent, and modest-looking young man called in, and spent an hour or two with Margaretta and her aunt. He did not present so imposing and showy an exterior as did Mr. Smith, but his conversation had in it far more substance and real common sense. After he had retired, Margaretta said—

"Well, it is no use; I cannot take any pleasure in the society of Thomas Fielding."

"Why not, my dear?" asked the aunt.

"Oh, I don't know; but he is so dull and prosy."

"I am sure he don't seem dull to me, Margaretta. He doesn't talk a great deal, it is true; but, then, what he does say is characterized by good sense, and evinces a discriminating mind."

"But don't you think, aunt, that my money has some influence in bringing him here?" And Margaretta looked up archly into her aunt's face.

"It may have, for aught I can tell. We cannot see the motives of any one. But I should be inclined to think that money would have little influence with Thomas Fielding, were not every thing else in agreement. He is, I think, a man of fixed and genuine principles."

"No doubt, aunt. But, still, I can't relish his society. And if I can't, I can't."

"Very true. If you can't enjoy his company, why you can't. But it cannot be, certainly, from any want, on his part, of gentlemanly manners, or kind attentions to you."

"No; but, then, he is so dull. I should die if I had no other company."

"Indeed, my child," Aunt Riston said, in a serious tone, "you ought to make the effort to esteem and relish the society of those who have evidently some stability of character, and whose conversation has in it the evidence of mature observation, combined with sound and virtuous principles, more than you do the flippant nonsense of mere ladies' men, or selfish, unprincipled fortune-hunters."

"Indeed, aunt, you are too severe on my favourites!" And Margaretta laughed gaily.

But to her aunt there was something sad in the sound of that laugh. It seemed like the knell of long and fondly cherished hopes.

"What do you think of Margaretta Riston, Mary?" asked Thomas Fielding of his sister, on the next evening after the visit just mentioned.

"Why do you ask so seriously, brother?" the sister said, looking into his face, with a smile playing about her lips.

"For a serious reason, sister. Can you guess what it is?"

"Perhaps so, and therefore I will not tax your modesty so far as to make you confess it."

"Very well, Mary. And now answer my question. What do you think of Margaretta?"

"I know nothing against her, brother."

"Nothing against her! Don't you know any thing in her favour?"

"Well, perhaps I do. She is said to be worth some fifty thousand dollars."

"Nonsense, Mary! What do I care about her fifty thousand dollars? Don't you know any thing else in her favour?"

"Why, yes, brother. As long as you seem so serious about the matter, I think Margaretta a fine girl. She is amiable in disposition—is well educated—tolerably good-looking, and, I think, ordinarily intelligent."

"Ordinarily intelligent!"

"Yes. Certainly there is nothing extraordinary about her."

"No, of course not."

"Well, brother, what next?"

"Why, simply, Mary, I like Margaretta very much. The oftener I see her, the more am I drawn towards her. To tell the plain, homely truth, I love her."

"And don't care any thing about her fifty thousand dollars?"

"No Mary, I don't think I do. Indeed, if I know my own feelings, I would rather she were not worth a dollar."

"And why so, Thomas?"

"Because, I fear the perverting influence of wealth on her mind. I am afraid her position will give her false views of life. I wish to marry for a *wife*—not for *money*. I can make money myself."

"Still, Thomas, Margaretta is, I think, an innocent-minded, good girl. I do not see that she has been much warped by her position."

"So she seems to me, and I am glad that my sister's observation corroborates my own. And now, Mary, do you think I have any thing to hope?"

"Certainly, I do."

"But why do you think so?"

"Because Margaretta must have good sense enough to see that you are a man of correct principles, and an affectionate disposition."

"Still, she may not see in me that which interests her sufficiently to induce her to marry me."

"That is true. But I don't believe you have any thing to fear."

"I cannot help fearing, Mary, for the simple reason, that I find my affections so much interested. A disappointment would be attended with extreme pain."

"Then I would end suspense at once."

"I will. To-morrow evening I will declare my feelings."

It was about nine o'clock on the next evening, while Mary Fielding sat reading by the centre-table, that her brother entered hastily, and threw himself upon the sofa, a deep sigh escaping him as he did so.

"What ails you, Thomas?" inquired his sister, rising and approaching him.

But he made no reply.

"Tell me, what ails you, Thomas?" Mary urged, taking his hand affectionately.

"I have been to see Margaretta," the brother at length replied, in as calm a voice as he could assume.

"And she has not, surely, declined your offer?"

"She has, and with what appeared to me an intimation that I loved her money, perhaps, better than herself."

"Surely not, brother!"

"To me it seemed so. Certainly she treated lightly my declaration, and almost jested with me."

The sister stood silent for some moments, and then said—

"The woman who could thus jest with you, Thomas, is unworthy of you."

"So I am trying to convince myself. But the trial is a deeply painful one."

And painful it proved for many weeks afterwards. But, finally, he was enabled to rise above his feelings.

In the mean time, Mr. Smith had wooed the heiress successfully, and, in doing so, his own heart had become interested, or, at least, he deceived himself into the belief that such was the case. He no longer jested, as he had done at first, about her money, nor declared, even to his friend Perkins, how strong an influence it had upon his affections. More serious thoughts of marriage had caused these selfish motives to retire out of sight and acknowledgment; but still they existed and still ruled his actions.

The aunt, when Margaretta made known to her that the young man had offered himself, was pained beyond measure, particularly as it was evident that her niece favoured the suitor.

"Indeed, Margaretta," said she, earnestly, "he is not worthy of you!"

"You judge him harshly, aunt," the niece replied. "I know him to be all that either of us could wish for."

"But how do you know, Margaretta?"

"I have observed him closely, and am sure that, I cannot be deceived in him."

"Alas! my child, if you know nothing beyond your own observation, you are far more ignorant than you suppose. Be guided, then, by me—trust more to my observation than your own. He is not the man to make you happy! Let me urge you, then, to keep him at a distance."

"I should do injustice to my own feelings, aunt, and to my own sense of right, were I to do so. In a word, and to speak out plainly, he offered himself last evening, and I accepted him!"

"Rash girl!" exclaimed Mrs. Riston, lifting her hands in astonishment and pain, "how could you thus deceive your best friend? How so sadly deceive yourself?"

"Do not distress yourself so, aunt. You have mistaken the character of Mr. Smith. He is, in every way, a different man from what you think him. He is altogether worthy of my regard and your confidence. I do not wish to deceive you, aunt; but you set yourself so resolutely against Mr. Smith from the first that I could not make up my mind to brave your opposition to a step which I was fully convinced it was right for me to take."

"Ah, Margaretta! You know not what you are doing. Marriage is a far more serious matter than you seem to think it. Look around among your young acquaintances, and see how many have wedded unhappily. And why? Because marriages were rushed into from a fond impulse, vainly imagined to be true affection. But no true affection can exist where there is not a mutual knowledge of character and qualities of mind. Now what do you know, really, about Mr. Smith? What does he know about you? Why, nothing! I want no stronger evidence of his unworthy motives, than the fact of his having offered himself after a three weeks' acquaintance. What could he know of you in that time? Surely not enough to be able to determine whether you would make him a suitable wife or not—enough, perhaps, to be satisfied of the amount of your wealth."

"You are unjust towards Mr. Smith," said Margaretta, half indignantly.

"Not half so unjust as he is towards you. But surely, my niece, you will reconsider this whole matter, and take full time to reflect."

"I cannot reconsider, aunt. My word is passed, and I would suffer any thing rather than break my word."

"You will suffer your heart to be broken, if you do not."

"Time will prove that!" and Margaretta tossed her head with a kind of mock defiance.

"Have you fixed your wedding day?" the aunt asked after a few moments' silence.

"Not yet. But Mr. Smith wants to be married in three weeks."

"In three weeks!"

"Yes; but I told him that I could not get ready within a month."

"A month! Surely you are not going to act so precipitately?"

One week after their marriage, Mr. Smith entered the room of his friend Mr. Perkins, with a pale, agitated countenance.

"What in the world has happened, Smith?" the friend asked, in alarm.

"Haven't you heard the news?"

"No. What news?"

"The United States Bank has failed!"

"Oh, no!"

"It is true. And every dollar of Margaretta's money is locked up there!"

"Really that is dreadful! I would sell the stock immediately for what it will bring, if I were you."

"So I wish to. But neither my wife nor her aunt are willing. And so soon after our marriage I do not like to use positive measures."

"But the case is urgent. Delay may sweep from you every dollar."

"So I fear. What shall I do then? To have the prize in hand, and find it thus suddenly escaping, is enough to drive me mad!"

"Sell in spite of them. That's my advice."

"I will!"

And the half crazy young fortune-hunter hurried away. In a few minutes after, he entered the room where sat his wife and her aunt in gloomy and oppressed silence.

"The best thing we can do, Margaretta, I am satisfied, is to sell," he said, taking a chair beside his wife. "The stock is falling every hour, and it is the opinion of competent judges that it will not be worth five dollars in a week."

"And other competent judges are of a very different opinion," replied the aunt. "Mr. Day, who was Margaretta's guardian, has just been here, and says that we must not sell by any means; that after the panic is over the stock will go up again. The bank, he assures us, is fully able to meet every dollar, and still have a large surplus. It would be folly then to sell, especially when there is no urgent demand for the money."

"There is more urgent demand than you know of," Mr. Smith said to himself with bitter emphasis. He added aloud,—

"Mr. Day may know something about the matter; but I am sure he is mistaken in the calculation he makes. It is said this morning, by those who know, that the assets of the bank are principally in worthless stocks, and that the shareholders will never get a cent. My advice, then, is to sell immediately; a bird in the hand is worth two in the bush."

But both the wife and aunt objected; and so soon after marriage he felt that positive opposition would come with a bad grace.

Steadily day after day, the stock went down, down, down—and day after day Mr. Smith persisted in having it sold. The fact was, duns now met him at every turn, and it was with the utmost difficulty that he could prevent his wife and her aunt from guessing at the nature of the many calls of his "particular friends." Money he must have, or he could not keep out of prison long, and the only chance for his obtaining money was in the sale of his wife's stock. But at the rates for which it was now selling, the whole proceeds would not cover the claims against him. At last, when the stock had fallen to twenty dollars, Mrs. Smith yielded to her husband's earnest persuasions, and handed him over the certificates of her stock, that he might dispose of them to the best possible advantage.

"Mr. Smith is late in coming home to his dinner," the aunt said, looking at the timepiece.

The young wife lifted her head from her hand, with a sigh, and merely responded,

"Yes, he is rather late."

"I wonder what keeps him so!" the old lady remarked, about five minutes after, breaking the oppressive silence.

"I'm sure I cannot tell. I gave him my certificates of stock to sell this morning."

"You did? I am afraid that was wrong, Margaretta."

"I'm sure I cannot tell whether it is or not, aunt. But I've had no peace about them, night nor day, since the bank failed."

There was bitterness in the tone of Margaretta's voice, that touched the feelings of her aunt, and tended to confirm her worst fears. But she could not, now, speak out plainly, as she had felt constrained to do before marriage, and therefore did not reply.

For more than an hour did the two women wait for the return of Mr. Smith, and then they went through the form of sitting down to the dinner-table. But few mouthfuls of food passed the lips of either of them.

Hour after hour moved slowly by, but still the husband of Margaretta appeared not; and when the twilight fell, it came with a strange uncertain fear to the heart of the young wife.

"What *can* keep him so late, aunt?" she said, anxiously, as the lights were brought in.

"Indeed, my child, I cannot tell. I hope that nothing is wrong."

"Wrong, aunt? What can be wrong?" and Margaretta looked her aunt eagerly and inquiringly in the face.

"I am sure, my child, I do not know. Something unusual must detain him, and I only hope that something may be evil neither to him nor yourself."

Again there was a deep and painful silence—painful at least to one heart, trembling with an undefinable sensation of fear.

"There he is!" ejaculated Margaretta springing to her feet, as the bell rang, and hurrying to the door before the servant had time to open it.

"Here is a letter for Mrs. Smith," said a stranger, handing her a sealed note, and then withdrawing quickly.

It was with difficulty that the young wife could totter back to the parlour, where she seated herself by the table, and with trembling hands broke the seal of the letter that had been given her. Her eyes soon took in the brief words it contained. They were as follow:—

"Farewell, Margaretta! We shall, perhaps, never meet again! Think of me as one altogether unworthy of you. I have wronged you—sadly wronged you, I know—but I have been driven on by a kind of evil necessity to do what I have done. Forget me! Farewell!"

This note bore neither date nor signature, but the characters in which it was written were too well known to be mistaken.

Mrs. Riston saw the fearful change that passed over the face of her niece as she read the note, and went quickly up to her. She was in time to save her from falling to the floor. All through the night she lay in a state of insensibility, and it was weeks before she seemed to take even the slightest interest in any thing that was going on around her.

It was about three o'clock of the day that Mr. Smith got possession of the certificates of deposit, that he entered the room of his friend, Perkins. He looked agitated and irresolute.

"Well, Smith, how are you?" his friend said. "Have you sold that stock yet?"

"Yes."

"Indeed! So you have triumphed over your wife's scruples. Well—what did you get for it?"

"Only eight thousand dollars."

"That was a shameful sacrifice!"

"Indeed it was. And it puts me into a terrible difficulty."

"What is that?"

"Why, I owe at least that sum; and I cannot stay here unless it is paid."

"That is bad."

"Out of the fifty thousand I could have squared up, and it would not have been felt. But I cannot use the whole eight thousand, and look Margaretta and her aunt in the face again. And if I don't pay my debts, you see, to prison I must go."

"You are in a narrow place, truly. Well, what are you going to do?"

"A question more easily asked than answered. Among my debts are about, four thousand dollars that must be paid whether or no."

"Why?"

"They are *debts of honour!*"

"Ah, indeed! that is bad. You will have to settle them."

"Of course!" Then, in a loud and emphatic whisper, he said—

"And I *have* settled them!"

"Indeed! Well, what next? How will you account to your wife for the deficiency?"

"Account to my wife!" and as he said this, he ground his teeth together, while his lip curled. "Don't talk to me in that way, Perkins, and cause me to hate the woman I have deceived and injured!"

"But what *are* you going to do, Smith?"

"I am going to clear out with the balance of the money in my pocket. I can't stay here, that's settled; and I'm not going away penniless, that's certain. Margaretta's old aunt has money enough, and can take care of her—so she's provided for. And I've no doubt but that she'll be happier without me than with me."

"Where are you going?"

"Somewhere down South."

"When?"

"At four o'clock this afternoon."

"Well, success to you. There are some rich widows in the Southern country, you know."

"I understand; but I'm rather sick of these operations. They are a little uncertain. But good-bye, and may you have better luck than your friend Smith."

"Good-bye." And the two young men shook hands cordially and parted.

At four o'clock Mr. Smith left for Baltimore—not the happiest man in the cars by a great deal.

Since that day the confiding young creature who had thrown all into the scale for him has neither seen him nor heard from him. To her the light of life seems fled for ever. Her face is very pale, and wears an expression of heart-touching misery. She is rarely seen abroad. Poor creature! In her one sad error, what a lifetime of sorrow has been involved!

Of all conditions in life, that of the young heiress, with her money in her own right, is peculiarly dangerous. The truly worthy shrink often from a tender of their affection, for fear their motives may be thought interested; while the mercenary push forward, and by well-directed flattery, that does not seem like flattery, win the prize they cannot appreciate.

There are such base wretches in society. Let those who most need to fear them be on their guard.

It is now but a few weeks since Thomas Fielding, who was despised and rejected by Margaretta, married a sweet girl in every way worthy of him. She is not rich in worldly goods, but she is rich in virtuous principles. The former Fielding does not need; but the latter he can cherish "as a holy prize."

IS MARRIAGE A LOTTERY?

"I AM afraid to marry," said a young lady, half jesting and half in earnest, replying to something a friend had said.

"Why so, Ella?" asked one of the company, who had thus far chosen rather to listen than join in the conversation of half a dozen gay young girls. She was a quiet, matronly-looking individual, some few years past the prime of life.

"For fear of being unhappy, Mrs. Harding," replied the first speaker.

"What an idea!" exclaimed a gay damsel, laughing aloud at the singular fear expressed by Ella. "For my part, I never expect to be happy until I am married."

"If marriage should make you any happier than you are now, Caroline, the result will be very fortunate. Your case will form an exception to the rule."

"Oh, no, Ella, don't say that," spoke up the one who had replied to her first remark. "Happiness is the rule, and unhappiness the exception."

"Then it happens strangely enough," returned Ella, smiling, "that we are more familiar with the exceptions than the rule."

"No, my dear, that cannot for a moment be admitted. Far more of happiness than misery results from marriage."

"Look at Ellen Mallory," was answered promptly, "and Mrs. Cummings, and half a dozen others I could name."

"The two you have mentioned are painful instances, I must admit, and form the exceptions of which I spoke; but the result is by no means one that should excite our surprise, for it is a natural consequence flowing from an adequate cause. If you marry as unwisely as did the persons you mention, I have no doubt but you will be quite as wretched as they are—it may be more so."

"I am sure Mr. Mallory is an elegant-looking man," said one of the company, "and might have had his pick among a dozen more attractive girls than ever Ellen Martine was."

"All as thoughtless and undiscriminating as she," remarked Mrs. Harding, quietly.

"Ellen is no fool," returned the last speaker.

"In the most important act of her whole life, she has certainly not shown herself to be a wise woman," said Mrs. Harding.

"But how in the world was she to know that Mr. Mallory was going to turn out so badly?" spoke up Ella.

"By opening her eyes, and using the ability that God has given her to see," was answered by Mrs. Harding.

"Those eyes are wondrous wise, I ween,
That see what is not to be seen,"

the maiden replied.

"Do you then really think, Ella," said Mrs. Harding, "that a young lady cannot make herself as thoroughly acquainted with a man's real qualities as to put any serious mistake in marriage entirely out of the question?"

"To me, I must confess that marriage seems very much like a lottery," answered Ella. "We may get a prize, but there are ten chances to one of our getting a blank."

"If you choose to make it a lottery, it will no doubt become so; but if entered into from right motives, there is no danger of this being the case."

"I don't know what you call right motives," said one; "but I'll tell you a necessary pre-requisite in the man who is to make me a husband."

"Well, child, what is it?"

"Plenty of money. I'm not going to be a poor man's wife, and work myself to death, all for love—no, not I!"

"I'll have a handsome man for a husband, or none," remarked another.

"Give me splendid talents," said a third.

"And what must you have, Ella?" asked Mrs. Harding, turning to the one she addressed.

"All three, if I can get them," replied Ella.

"Beauty, wealth, and talents. These you think would satisfy you?"

"Oh, yes; I should be rather hard to please if they did not."

"Let me relate to you the histories of two friends of mine who married young," said Mrs. Harding, without remarking upon what had just been declared. "Perhaps they may contain lessons that it will be of use for you all to get by heart."

"Oh, yes, do!" said the young ladies, gathering around Mrs. Harding, who, after a short pause, related what follows.

"In my younger days," began Mrs. Harding, "I had two intimate friends, to whom I was warmly attached. I loved them for their many good qualities, and particularly for their unselfishness. To make others happy, always appeared to give them a double pleasure. They were nearly of the same age, and possessed equal external advantages; but their characters were very different. Sarah Corbin, who was a few months older than her friend and almost constant companion, Harriet Wieland, was quiet, thoughtful, and observant; while Harriet, who had great personal attractions, never appeared to look beneath the surface. She believed every thing to be true that bore the semblance of truth, to her all that glittered was gold. Like you, and most other young ladies, we sometimes talked of marriage, and the qualifications desirable in a good husband. Harriet, whether in a gay or sober mood, always declared, like Ella here, that he who won her heart must have riches, manly beauty, and brilliant talents. These she called man's cardinal virtues. Sarah never had much to say on these matters, and, when we asked her opinion, she generally replied evasively.

"A young man named Eaverson, answering pretty nearly to the beau ideal of Harriet Wieland, came from a neighbouring city to reside in this. He was connected with a wealthy and highly respectable family, was really a handsome man, and possessed very fine abilities. He had studied law, and opened his office here for the purpose of pursuing it as a regular profession; but, not meeting with much practice at first, he occupied a large portion of his time in literary pursuits, writing for the magazines and reviews. He also published a small volume of poetry, which contained many really brilliant specimens of verse.

"Circumstances threw Eaverson into the circle of which we formed a part, and we were consequently introduced to him. In the course of time, he began to pay rather marked attentions to Sarah Corbin, at which I felt a little surprised, as he had met Harriet Wieland quite as often, and she was far more beautiful and showy, and more likely, it seemed to me, to attract one like him than the other. Either Sarah was unconscious that his attentions were more marked in her case, or she did not wish her observation of the fact to be known, for all our allusions to the subject were evaded with a seeming indifference that left our minds in doubt. Such were our impressions at first; but the sequel showed that she had marked his first advances with lively interest, and understood their meaning quite as well as we did.

"About Eaverson there was every thing to attract the heart of a maiden not well guarded; and Sarah found that it required the fullest exercise of her reason to prevent her from letting every affection of her mind go out and attach itself to an object that seemed, at first sight, so worthy of her love. But by nature and from education she was thoughtful and observant; and a wise mother had taught her that in marriage external accomplishments and possessions were nothing, unless united with virtuous principles and well-regulated passions. The brilliant attractions of Eaverson strongly tempted her to take his moral fitness for granted; but wiser counsels prevailed in her mind; and with a vigorous hand laid upon her heart to keep down its errant impulses, she exercised, with coolness and a well-balanced mind, the powers of discrimination which God had given for her guidance through life."

All the time that this process was going on in her mind, we remained in ignorance of the fact that she ever thought of the young man, except when he was present, or his name introduced by others. To her, all that related to marriage was too serious to form the theme of ordinary conversation, light jests, or idle chit-chat. Rarely indeed would she have any thing to say, when others spoke lightly or jested on the subject. This being the case, now that her own mind had become deeply interested in a matter of most vital importance to her future welfare, she had no one to disturb the even balance of her reflections by a thoughtless word, an untimely jest, or a false opinion flowing from inexperience or a want of ability to read human nature aright. Silently, freely, and with no biassing influence, in the unapproachable chambers of her own thoughts did she weigh the real character of Eaverson, as far as she could understand it, against what was merely external and personal. The more marked the attentions of the young man became, the more earnestly did she seek to comprehend his real character. Every word he uttered in her presence, every sentiment he expressed, every action and every look were closely scanned, and their meaning, as having reference to principles in the mind, sought to be understood. Such careful scrutiny did not go unrewarded. When Eaverson, soon after her mind was made up in regard to him, made an offer of his hand, the offer was unhesitatingly declined. Sarah had seen enough to satisfy her, that with all his talents, beauty, and wealth, he was wanting in virtuous principles and a high sense of honour.

"I confess, that, with others, I was greatly surprised when the fact of Sarah's having declined the hand of Eaverson became known. The selection of her by one like him seemed so high a preference, and such a marked tribute to her worth and virtue, that it was scarcely credible that she could have remained indifferent to his love. But she saw deeper than we did."

"'I cannot understand the reason of your refusal to accept Mr. Eaverson's offer?' I said to Sarah, one day, when the conversation took a turn that gave me an opportunity of alluding to the subject. 'Do you know any thing against him?'

"'Nothing further than the conclusions of my own mind, arising from a careful observation of his sentiments, manners, and unguarded expressions,' she replied.

"'Was it from such conclusions that you declined his offer?'

"'From these alone, for I know nothing of his history before he came to this city, and nothing of his life since he has been here.'

"'May you not possibly be mistaken?'

"'No. From the moment he seemed in the least pleased with me, I commenced observing him closely. It was not long before I heard him utter a sentiment, while speaking to another, that showed him to possess very false views of life in at least one particular. This I noted, and laid it by in my memory for comparison with any thing else I might see or hear.'

"'But you would not condemn a man for having erroneous views of life?' said I.

"'Oh, no; not if his principles be pure. But if false views arise from a perverted heart, then I would condemn the man. What I heard, I noticed in order to determine, if possible, from what source it came. A very long time did not pass, before I saw something that told me very plainly that the false view which I have mentioned depended more upon a perversion of the heart than an error in the understanding. I likewise discovered, very soon, that when in conversation with me, he was, evidently, more upon his guard, as to what sentiments he declared, than he was when in conversation with others. But I need not state particularly the whole process by which I arrived at conclusions sufficiently clear to warrant my full and prompt rejection of his suit.'

"'In what estimation do you hold him?' I asked.

"'As a man without honour or virtue,' she said, decidedly.

"'That is a broad and severe judgment,' I replied.

"'So it is. I have made it for myself. Of course, I cannot expect others to view him in the same light; nor do I believe many others would form this conclusion from the evidences that were presented to my mind. But, as for me, I have no doubt on the subject. Rather than become his wife, I would suffer death; for a union with him would be, to me, the depth of misery.'

"The seriousness with which Sarah spoke satisfied me that she believed all she said, and had, at some cost of feeling, rejected an offer of marriage that would have been an exceedingly desirable one, had the character of the man who made it been fully approved.

"A short time after the rejection of his suit by Miss Corbin, I noticed that Eaverson appeared more inclined to keep company with Harriet Wieland than before. I could not help feeling regret at this, for, notwithstanding I thought Sarah had judged the young man rather severely, I was yet satisfied that there must be some ground for her conclusions in regard to his character. Slight attentions, encouraged by Harriet, soon became the bold advances of a lover. A few months after his suit had been declined by Sarah, he offered himself to her friend, and was unhesitatingly accepted.

"In the mean time, a young man, whom I will call Williamson, had met Sarah occasionally, and showed a disposition to win, if possible, her favourable regard. His exterior was by no means elegant; his literary attainments were not great; nor was he in the enjoyment of any thing beyond a moderate income. Place him and Eaverson in almost any company, and the latter would nearly hide him from view. But, with the most moderate pretensions, and unattractive exterior, Williamson's character was formed upon a ground-work of good sense and virtuous principles. He had little facility of expression, but he thought clearly, and, in most things, acted from a sound judgment. He was much pleased with Sarah before Eaverson attempted to gain her affections; and noticed his advances. For the result he looked with some interest. When it became clearly apparent that she had thrown him off, Williamson was satisfied that she was a girl of discrimination and sound sense, and immediately resolved that he would know her better. The oftener he met her, and the nearer he observed her, the more excellent did her character seem in his eyes. The result was an offer of marriage, which was accepted by Sarah, as much to our surprise as was her rejection of Eaverson.

"My two young friends were married about the same time. The wedding of Harriet was a brilliant one, and she was the envy of dozens of young girls who had hoped and tried to make a conquest of the man who had chosen to unite his fortunes with hers. Sarah's nuptials were celebrated in a less imposing manner, and created but little sensation. Most of her friends thought she had done but poorly. Whether this were so, will be seen in the sequel.

"Harriet, with all her want of reflection and in-sight into character, was a young woman of strong feelings, and loved, when she did love, with something like blind idolatry. Thus she loved her husband. He was every thing to her, and she believed him as near perfection as a mortal could well be. The first few months of her married life passed swiftly away in the enjoyment of as high a degree of felicity as her mind seemed capable of appreciating. After that, a shadow fell upon her spirit—dim and almost imperceptible at first, but gradually becoming denser and more palpable. Harriet had noticed, from the first, that her husband but rarely spoke of his family, and always evaded any questions that a natural curiosity prompted her to make. If he received any letter from home, he carefully concealed the fact from her. The wealth, respectability, and high standing of his family made Harriet, as a matter of course, feel desirous of bearing a more intimate relation to its members than she now did. The more she thought about this, the less satisfied did she feel. It was the marked dislike manifested by her husband to any reference to his family, that first caused a coldness to pass over the heart of the young wife, and a shadow to dim the bright sunshine of her spirits; for it induced the thought that something might be wrong. Once give such a thought birth, and let mystery and doubt continue to harass the mind, and peace is gone for ever. A thousand vague suspicions will enter, and words, looks, and actions will have a signification never apparent before.

"Thus it was with my young friend, ere six months had passed since her wedding-day. To increase her anxious doubts, her husband seemed to grow cold towards her. This might all be imagination, but the idea, once in possession of her mind, found numberless sustaining evidences. He went out more frequently in the evening and stayed out later than at first. Sometimes he would sit silent and abstracted, and only reply in monosyllables to her questions or remarks.

"One day he came home to dinner, looking graver than usual. But, during the meal, there was an evident desire on his part to appear cheerful and unconcerned; he talked more freely than usual, and even made many light and jesting remarks. But the veil assumed was too thin. Harriet's eyes saw through it, and rested only upon the sombre reality beneath. As they were rising from the table, he said,

"'Harriet, dear! I must run on to New York this afternoon, on business. The interest of a client in a large estate there requires my immediate presence in that city.'

"Eaverson did not look his wife steadily in the face as he said this although he plainly tried to do so. But this she did not remark at the time. Her mind only rested upon the fact of his going away.

"'How long will you be gone?' she asked in a choking voice.

"'I will try and be back to-morrow. If not, you will at least see me home on the day after.'

"'Why can't I—'

"She paused—her eyes fell to the floor, and the colour deepened on her cheeks.

"'What, dear?'

"'Go with you?'

"It was in New York that the family of Eaverson resided.

"'Not now,' he quickly answered. 'I am compelled to go in too much hurry; but the next time business takes me there you shall accompany me.'

"Nothing could be more unsatisfactory than this. Was she not to be introduced to his family, as his wife, formally? Was she only to go to the city of their residence at some future time, when business called her husband there? The thought caused a chill to pass through her frame. She made no reply. But the paleness that overspread her face, and the sadness that fell upon her countenance, revealed to her husband, too plainly, her state of mind. He said nothing, however, to dispel the gloom she felt. Words, he no doubt felt, would be fruitless.

"The young wife parted with her husband it tears, and then retired to her chamber, where she gave way to a paroxysm of grief, that had its origin more in the accompanying mystery than in the fact of her husband's absence. I say mystery, for she did not fully credit the reason he had given for his hurried visit to New York, and felt that there was a mystery connected with it, that, somehow or other, deeply affected her happiness.

"After the mind of Harriet had grown calmer, she commenced restoring to order the few articles in her chamber that had been disarranged in the hurried preparation made by her husband for his departure. As she was about placing the coat he had worn in the morning, and which he had changed for another on going away, in the wardrobe, her hand pressed against a letter in one of the pockets, which a sudden curiosity tempted her to read. The direction was in a small, delicate hand, and the post-mark New York. Hurriedly opening it, when she saw this, she read its brief contents, which were as follow:

"DEAR HENRY—I heard, indirectly, within the last hour, that you were married. I cannot believe it, yet the thought has maddened me! If you do not come to me by to-morrow night, I will go to you on the following day—for the truth or falsity of what I have heard must be verified to me at once. If it be true—God help the innocent heart you have betrayed, and most cruelly wronged. It can only break!

"ADELAIDE."

"The trembling hands of the horror-stricken wife could hold the fatal epistle no longer than to permit her eyes to rest upon the signature. It then fell rustling to the floor, and she sat pale, quivering in every nerve, and unconscious of any thing but a wild whirling of all her senses.

"It was my fortune, or misfortune, to call upon my young friend just at this time. I was told that she was in her chamber; and, as our intimacy was very great, I took a liberty we were in the habit of taking with each other, and went up to her, unannounced. My gentle tap at her door not being answered, I opened it and went in. As I have just described her, thus I found her. My entrance but partially restored her self-command. She stared wildly at me, stretched out her hands, and made an effort to speak. I sprang toward her, and she fell forward against my bosom, with a deep groan that made me shudder. Thus she lay for nearly five minutes as still as a statue. Then a slight quiver ran through her frame, which was followed by a gush of tears. For a long time she continued weeping and sobbing, but at length grew calmer. All this time I could see an open letter lying upon the floor, which I doubted not was the caused of this distressing scene. When the self-command of Harriet was at last restored, and she began to reflect upon the consequences likely to flow from another's witnessing the wild agitation she had displayed, a shade of anxious confusion passed over her face. At this moment her eye rested upon the fatal letter, which she caught up eagerly and concealed. I asked no question, nor made any remarks. She looked at me steadily for a moment, and then let her eyes fall thoughtfully to the floor.

"'You are surprised and confounded, no doubt,' she at length said, mournfully, 'at what you have seen. Pardon me if I refrain from mentioning the cause. It is one of which I cannot speak.'

"I begged her not to reveal the cause of her affliction, if to do so were at all in violation of what she deemed right; but to accept my deepest sympathies, and to put it in my power, if that were possible, to mitigate, in some degree, the pain of mind she was suffering.

"'That you cannot do,' said she. 'It is beyond the reach of human aid.'

"'May Heaven, then, give you strength to bear it,' I returned, with emotion.

"'Heaven only can,' she replied in a subdued voice.

"I could say no more, for my ignorance of the cause of her distress put it out of my power to offer consolation, more particularly as it was her expressed wish that I should remain in ignorance. I staid an hour with her, during which time I learned that her husband had been suddenly called to New York on business. It was one of the unhappiest hours I ever spent in my life. On going away, I could not help recalling the conversation I had once held with Sarah Corbin about Mr. Eaverson, nor help feeling that there might be too much truth in her declarations that she believed him to be a man without honour or virtue. There was no doubt in my mind that Harriet's distress was in some way connected with her husband's absence, and it occurred to me that the letter I had seen upon the floor, and which she concealed so eagerly, might not have been intended for her eyes, and might contain things which for her to know would be fatal to her peace through life. In this, my conjectures were of course true.

"I called in to see Mrs. Eaverson on the next day, reluctantly, but from a sense of duty. I found her calm, but pale, and with a look of distress. She said but little. No allusion whatever was made to the condition in which I had found her on the previous afternoon. I sat only half an hour, and then went away. I could not stay longer, for my presence seemed oppressive to her, and hers was equally so to me.

"On the third day succeeding that on which Mr. Eaverson went to New York, I saw a newspaper paragraph headed, 'Melancholy Circumstances.' It related, briefly, that the daughter of respectable and wealthy parents in New York had been deeply wronged about a year previous by an unprincipled cousin, whom she passionately loved. The consequence was, that the young man had to leave the city, under the promise of never returning to it, unless he consented to marry his cousin. This penalty was imposed by the father of the girl, who declared his intention to shoot him if he ever saw him in New York. The result of this baseness on the part of the young man was the utter estrangement of his family. They threw him off entirely. But, as he had a handsome fortune in his own right, and the cause of his removal from New York did not become generally known, he soon found his way into the best society in a neighbouring city. Some months afterwards he married a lovely girl, who was all unconscious of the base retch into whose keeping she had given the inestimable jewel of her love. A few days since, the narration proceeded, the cousin, by some means or other, obtained a knowledge of this fact. She wrote to him demanding an interview, and threatening that if she did not obtain one in twenty-four hours, she would immediately come to him and ascertain for herself, if what she had heard were true. Alarmed for the peace of his bride, the young man hurried on to New York, and, at the risk of his life, gained an interview with the lovely girl he had so deeply injured. He did not attempt to conceal the fact of his marriage, but only urged the almost broken-hearted victim of his base dishonour not to do anything that could bring to his wife a knowledge of his conduct, as it must for ever destroy her peace. This confession blasted at once and for ever all the poor girl's hopes. She gave her betrayer one long, fixed, intense look of blended agony, reproach, and shame, and then, without uttering a word, retired slowly from his presence. She sought her mother, who, from the first, had rather drawn her into her very bosom than thrown her off harshly, and related what she had just heard. She shed no tear, she uttered no reproach, but simply told what her mother had known for months too well. That night her spirit left its earthly habitation. Whether she died of a broken heart, or by her own hands, is not known. The family sought not to investigate the cause,—to them it was enough to know that she was dead and at peace.

"Whether this statement ever met the eye of Mrs. Eaverson is more than I can tell. I did not venture to call upon her after I had seen it. A few weeks subsequently I met her in the street on the arm of her husband. She was sadly changed, and had the appearance of one just recovering from a long and severe illness. Eaverson himself had a look of suffering.

"The notoriety given by the publication of the acts of his base conduct in New York caused Eaverson to feel little at ease in this city. Some months afterwards he removed to the South with his wife, much against the wishes of her friends. Harriet did not want to go, but she could do no less than accompany her husband.

"Some three years afterwards, it was whispered about that Harriet had left her husband and returned home to her father; but that the matter was kept very quiet, and that she had not been seen by any of her old friends. It was said, that after living some time at the South, Mr. Eaverson grew indifferent towards his wife. A virtuous woman, she could not but be deeply shocked on discovering her husband's want of virtue. This she could not conceal; and its appearance was a standing reproof and condemnation of his principles and conduct. No bad man could endure this. Its effect would be certain estrangement. From dislike towards his wife, his feelings gradually deepened into hatred. Open abuse soon followed neglect; when she fled from him, with two young children, and sought the protection of her father's house.

"It was nearly a year after Harriet's return, before I saw her. I could hardly believe, when I did meet her and grasp her hand, that the pale, dejected, care-worn being who stood before me was the same with the light-hearted, beautiful, gay young girl I had known but a few years back. Alas! how surely does pain of mind forestall the work of time!

"A few days after this meeting, which made me sad for weeks, I spent an afternoon and evening with Mrs. Williamson, formerly Sarah Corbin. She had two children, a boy and a girl, and was living somewhat secluded, but with every comfort she could desire. Her husband was a merchant in a good business. When he came home at tea-time and met his wife, it was with one of those quiet but genuine smiles that you know come from the heart. He welcomed me, as he always did, with great cordiality; and then calling for Sarah, his eldest child, who ran in from the next room the instant she heard his vice, he took her upon his lap, and, after kissing her with great tenderness, asked and answered a dozen little questions to her great delight. At tea-time Mr. Williamson conversed more freely than was usual with him when I was present. I noticed, as I had often done before, that, on whatever subject he spoke, his remarks, though few, were full of good sense, and indicative of close observation. The slightest deviation from honour or integrity met with his decided condemnation, while virtuous actions were as warmly approved. I could perceive, from the expression of his wife's face, and the tones of her voice when she spoke, that she not only held her husband in high estimation, but loved him with a tenderness that had grown with years. Qualities of mind and heart, not external attractions, such as brilliant accomplishments, beauty, or wealth, had drawn her towards him at first: these had won her young affections, and they had become purer and brighter, and increased in attractive power as year after year went by.

"On going home that evening, I could not help pausing and looking back. Vividly, as it were but yesterday, came up before my mind my two young friends when, as maidens, their hands were sought in wedlock. I remembered how one, with true wisdom, looked below the imposing exterior and sought for moral worth as the basis of character in him who asked her hand; while the other, looking no deeper than the surface, was dazzled by beauty, wealth, and talents. The result you all have seen."

Mrs. Harding paused in the narrative. Half a dozen eager voices instantly inquired the ultimate fate of Mrs. Eaverson. "A few years after her return home," resumed the narrator, "she died. Her husband during that period neither wrote to her nor visited her. What has become of him I don't know. Mrs. Williamson is still living, surrounded by a lovely family of children. Her oldest daughter has just been married, and, to all present appearances, has united her fate with one every way worthy of her hand. Mr. Williamson, or rather Mr. Rierdon, as I should truly have called him, you all know."

"Mr. Rierdon!" exclaimed Ella. "It can't be possible you mean him?"

"Not old Mr. Rierdon!" exclaimed another. "Why he is respected and loved by every one!"

"I know he is," returned Mrs. Harding, "and well deserves to be. Yet, when a young man, he had nothing very imposing about him, and was thought of but little account by a set of young and foolish girls, just such as you are, whose heads were liable to be turned by any dashing young fellow with more impudence than brains, or more talent than principle, who happened to thrust himself forward and push better men aside. I hope the lesson I have endeavoured to teach you may not be lost entirely; and that when any one of you has an offer of marriage, she will look rather at the heart than the head—at the qualities instead of the accomplishments—of him who makes it. If she does not, she will be in great danger of committing the sad mistake made by my excellent but thoughtless young friend, Harriet Wieland, of whom I never can think without pain."

Whether the narrative of Mrs. Harding had any good effect upon her hearers, we do not know; but we would fain believe that it had; and we hope our fair young readers will not forget the important lesson it teaches. Let them be well assured that marriage is no lottery, except where it is made so. Every one who will look at the moral qualities of the object of her regard, instead of at what is merely external, will see deep enough to enable her to come to a right decision in regard to him. There is no necessity for mistakes in marriage.

THE UNLOVED ONE.

AN EXTRACT FROM "LOVE IN HIGH LIFE."

......FIXED in his resolution to repel every manifestation of tenderness on the part of his wife, Percy Edwards maintained towards her the same cold formality, in spite of all her earnest efforts to break the icy crust of his feelings. He did not love her, and was not inclined to affect a passion; nay, she was absolutely repulsive to him, and the least he could do, under the circumstances, was to protect himself as he did without overt acts of unkindness.

And thus disjoined, instead of united, Mr. and Mrs. Edwards moved along their way through life, envied by hundreds, who, in exchanging with them, would have left an Eden of happiness for a dreary wilderness.

A few months of such an existence completely broke down the spirits of Kate. She had no pride to sustain her. Thousands, as unloved as she, seek refuge in pride, pleasure, and a heartless worship at the gilded shrine of fashion. They meet coldness with a sharp disdain; and, finding nothing to love at home, turn to what the world has to offer, and become mere bubbles on the surface of society—prominent, brilliant, and useless. Nay, worse than useless; for they reflect the light of heaven falsely, and create discontent in those who see only their glittering exterior, and vainly imagine it to be the correspondent of internal delight.

It was not so with Kate; for she was sincere, unselfish, and true-hearted, and could not seek a false pleasure, when the sources of real delight became dry. A naiad, at a fountain, the waters of which had failed, she turned not to another, but bent weeping over the spot, hoping, yet faint with a long desire to hear the murmur of the coming stream.

There fell, at last, a gleam of light across her path. In her dark and cloudy sky arched, beautifully, a bow of promise. Hope, faint, yet sweet to her spirit, revived, and she looked to the future with a trembling heart. For a long time she locked in her own thoughts the dear secret she had discovered and pondered over it with a daily increasing pleasure. Then it was whispered, low and with a blushing cheek, to her husband. She was to become a mother!

From that moment she felt that there was a change. From that moment her husband's manner was different. He was still as polite and formal as, before; but with these was blended a something that her heart interpreted as tenderness for his wife; and from this her fainting spirit drew the aliment that sustained it. If, suddenly coming upon her now, he surprised her weeping, he did not turn away, silent and cold, as before; but would speak some word of apparent sympathy, which instantly dried up the fountains of grief. And thus the time passed, until another being saw the light—until another voice sounded upon the air. Oh! with what a thrill of delight did the young mother take her new-born babe into her arms, and hail it as the bond that was to bind to hers the heart of her husband. How eagerly did she read the face of that husband—as he bent over and gazed upon the innocent being to which she had given birth—and marked its glow of pleasure. But, he did not look into *her* face—he had eyes *only for his boy!* The mother sighed faintly; but he did not hear the sigh. Her long lashes fell slowly upon her cheeks, and tears stole from beneath them; but he turned away without observing she wept.

The bow of promise, which had spanned the heaven of her mind, faded away; and the light that had lain so warmly upon her path grew dim. There was love in the heart of her husband only for his child, but none for her. That dreadful truth came with a shock, felt to the very centre of her being; and, reacting upon her exhausted system, disturbed all its vital functions. Fever and delirium laid their hands upon her, and for many days the light of life but flickered in the wind that seemed every moment about to extinguish it.

When, at last, through the skill of her physician, the disease abated, and health, though feeble, began to flow once more through her veins; and when reason came back, and with it the outgushing tenderness of the young mother, she found that her babe had been laid upon another breast, and that from another it was to draw the sustenance which nature had supplied for it in her own bosom.

Against this her heart arose in instant rebellion. But no freedom of choice was left her. The physician said that her health was too slender to admit of the exhaustion attendant upon nursing her own babe. The husband would not hear of such a thing for a moment. And her husband's mother older-hearted and more worldly-minded than even he, openly sneered at the idea of one in her position degrading herself into a mere child's nurse!

It was all in vain that Kate pleaded, tearfully, for the mother's highest privilege. Those who had the power forced her into a compliance with their will; and the fountain in her bosom, that stirred at the voice of her babe, was suffered to become dry.

From that time, the health of Mrs. Edwards visibly declined; or, rather, was never restored to its previous condition. She became subject to fainting fits and long periods of depression, from which nothing could arouse her. The babe, instead of forming a link between her and her husband, became a rival in his affections. Mr. Edwards worshipped his boy; but, for his wife, had no feeling other than indifference, if not absolute dislike. All this Kate saw; and it extinguished her last and dearest hope.

To those who could only look upon the surface, Mr. Edwards was regarded as one of the kindest and most attentive of husbands; and when a rumour of his wife's fits of gloomy depression of spirits went abroad, the fault was attributed to herself, and laid to the charge of a naturally capricious and dissatisfied temper.

"If she had fewer of life's blessings," said one, "she would be happier. The very surplus of every thing makes her appetite pall."

"Any woman, situated as she is," remarked another, "who is not contented, deserves to be wretched. I have no sympathy for her. Her husband I know very well, and know him to be one of the kindest and most indulgent of men."

"He has indulged her too much," alleged another.

These impressions the elder Mrs. Edwards strengthened and confirmed, whenever she had occasion to say any thing on the subject.

"Percy has rather a gloomy time of it," she would sometimes remark, when allusion was made to the subject; and then, when the inquisitive would ask as to the cause of Kate's strange conduct, she would shake her head gravely, and say—

"Over-indulgence has spoiled her."

Or—

"It's hard to tell what ails her, unless it be the desire for some impossible thing. Some minds are never content. To multiply their blessings is but to multiply their misery."

Or—

"Heaven knows what ails her! Percy would give worlds for that knowledge, if with it came also the remedy."

The rapid decline in his wife's health, or rather its failure, after the birth of her child, to come back its old standard united to her lowness of spirits—naturally gave her husband some concern, and he consulted her physician as to the cause. He, as the profession generally do, assigned a physical cause, and recommended change of air.

"Let her go to the sea-shore, or among the Mountains," said he.

And this change was proposed to Kate.

"I saw Doctor R—to-day," said her husband, after the interview, "and he recommends a few weeks on the sea-shore, or somewhere among the mountains."

"I don't wish to go," replied Kate, in a low, sad voice.

"But your health, Kate," said Mr. Edwards.

"I shall be just as well at home," she replied.

"No, I will not admit that. Doctor R—is sure that a change of air will do you good; and what he says is reasonable."

Kate made no answer. Mr. Edwards continued to urge the matter upon her; but she had no more to say.

On the same evening Percy called to see his mother.

"How is Kate?" inquired the latter.

"No better. I saw Doctor R—about her to-day, and he says a change of air is absolutely necessary, and recommends a few weeks at the Bedford Springs, or at Newport, or Cape May."

"No doubt it would do her much good."

"No doubt in the world. But, as in every thing else of late, she is opposed to just what her friends recommend to her as best."

"She doesn't want to go?"

"No, of course not."

"Did you tell that the doctor recommended the change?"

"Yes. But she insists upon it that she will be just as well at home."

"A compliment to the medical opinion of Doctor R—!

"Isn't it? I wish you would see her, and urge her to go somewhere."

"Very well; though I don't know that what I say will be of much use. I am not one of her favourites."

"See her, at any rate. It won't do to let her sink down and die, as she certainly will if something cannot be done to arouse her."

"I will call upon Mrs. Harrison and tell her what the doctor says. She has great influence over her; and can persuade her to go if any one can."

The mother of Kate heard what the doctor had said, and approved of his recommendation. She knew, better than any one else, the true nature of the disease from which her daughter was suffering; and, although she did not hope for much from a change of scene, yet she believed the effect would be salutary rather than otherwise. So she went to see her immediately. She found her, as usual, alone in her chamber, with a sad countenance, and a drooping, listless air. After inquiring, tenderly, about her health, she said—

"I understand that Doctor R—recommends a change of air."

"What all doctors recommend when they do not know the cause and nature of a disease," replied Kate, with a faint smile.

"But I think, with Doctor R—, that a few weeks at the sea-shore will be of great benefit. The change will interest your mind as well as invigorate your body."

"A temporary benefit may be derived from such a change," said Kate; "but it cannot be permanent. When I return, I will sink again; and, perhaps, lower, from the unnatural excitement to which I have been subjected."

"Kate, my child, it is wrong for you to give up in this way. Your disease is more of the mind than of the body; and you have the power to arouse yourself and throw it off, if you will."

"The power, mother! I, the power!" exclaimed Kate, in a voice that made her mother start.

"Have you not?" inquired Mrs. Harrison calmly.

"Has the bird, whose wing is broken, the power to fly?" asked Kate.

"Unless you make an effort to throw off your present state of mind, you cannot live. And are you willing to die, and leave this dear child in the hands of those who cannot love it as you do?"

"Has it not already been taken from me? Does it not draw its existence from another breast?"

"But your health required—"

"My health! mother! My very life depended upon the privilege you have all denied me. Do you want the proof? Look at that shadowy hand"—and she held up the thin white member against the light, which almost shone through it—"and at this shrunken face," and she laid her hand upon her colourless cheek. "Restore the fountain that has been dried, and let my babe drink at it, and there is some hope. None without."

"That is impossible, Kate"—

"And just as impossible is my return to health through the means proposed."

"But, for the sake of your friends, you ought to be willing to try the means of restoration prescribed by a physician in whom we all have confidence."

"Friends?" said Kate, half to herself. "Friends? Have I any friends?"

"My child, why do you speak in this way?" asked her mother, in a voice half sorrowful, half reproving.

"*Friends* seek your good, not their own pleasure," continued Kate. "Have I any who may be called by so excellent a name?"

And she shook her head mournfully.

"Have you not a husband?" said Mrs. Harrison.

Kate again shook her head; and then, after a pause, replied—

"There is a man who calls himself my husband; but he is so only in name."

"Kate! Kate!" exclaimed her mother, "are you mad? How dare you utter such language?"

"A heart that is breaking, mother," said the unhappy creature, "may be pardoned, if, in a moment of intense suffering, it is betrayed into an expression of pain."

A long and gloomy silence followed this remark, which smote with the apparent force of a hammer upon the heart of Mrs. Harrison. No further attempt was made, at the time, to induce Kate to yield to the wishes of her friends. Her mother endeavoured, rather, to draw off her mind from thoughts such as those to which she had just given utterance. But, she was none the less deeply impressed with the belief that the change proposed would be beneficial; nor did she intend abandoning her efforts to induce her daughter to go from home for a short season. At the first opportunity she had an interview with Mr. Edwards, and held a conference with him on the subject of Kate's mental disease. She found him rather reserved, and disinclined to much conversation on the subject. But, on pressing the matter upon him, he was more free to say what was in his mind. To her expressions of concern for Kate, he responded with much apparent earnestness; said that it gave him great concern, and that he was satisfied she could not live over a few years if some change did not take place.

"Since the birth of her child," said he, "she has never regained her strength. That dangerous fever gave her system a terrible shock."

"I'm afraid," returned her mother, "that we erred in not permitting her to nurse her child—what she so earnestly desired to do. She cannot, it seems, get over that."

"She has never said so to me."

"But no later than yesterday she alluded to it while I talked with her, and in a way that satisfied me of her having taken the matter far more deeply to heart than I had imagined."

"That is a weakness, as you must yourself see, Mrs. Harrison. Apart from considerations of health, I would not have my wife a mere wet nurse; and I am surprised that she should have thought of such a thing."

"The desire was but a natural one," replied Mrs. Harrison. "As to there being any thing degrading in the act of a mother giving nourishment to her own babe, as some strangely enough seem to think, I cannot see it. I drank at my mother's breast, and my child, in turn, drank at mine; and, I believe, it would have been far better for Kate at this moment if she had done the same for her own off-spring. In this matter, people are going against nature; and whenever this is done, evil of some kind must inevitably follow."

"But, Mrs. Harrison," returned Edwards, "her state of health puts this out of the question. You know that she was dangerously ill, and that if a nurse had not been provided for the child, it would have died."

"I know all that. But, when the sudden illness abated, and she was able to give nourishment to her babe, all, with one accord, denied her a mother's privilege, though she plead for it day after day with tears. Ah, Percy! I fear a great and irreparable wrong was then done."

"It may be so. But I cannot believe but that we acted rightly. Our motives were at least good."

"No one doubts that."

"I am sure, if she would consent to leave home for a few weeks, her health would improve," said Percy Edwards.

"It would, no doubt, benefit her. But she has an unconquerable reluctance to going. Still, I think we may induce her to do as we wish. Only we must act towards her with great tenderness. I am afraid—pardon me for speaking plainly—that you do not consider, sufficiently, her weak state. She needs to be treated with the gentleness and affection that we show to a child."

Mr. Edwards looked surprised at this remark.

"I am sure, Mrs. Harrison," he replied, "no man could do more for the happiness of a woman, than I do for that of Kate. How I could act differently is more than I can imagine."

"It may be natural to you, Mr. Edwards," said Mrs. Harrison, "but you are wanting in that tenderness of manner so grateful, nay, so essential to the heart of a wife."

"I am!"

"I speak plainly, because the necessity for doing so is imperative. Your manner towards Kate has ever been respectful, polite, attentive, but not affectionate; and without the latter, the former never can satisfy the heart of a loving woman. I do not blame you for this. It may all be natural; but I feel it to be my duty to speak of it now, and to suggest, at least temporarily, a change."

Mr. Edwards did not reply for some moments. He then said—

"Mrs. Harrison, I must own that what you allege surprises me. You charge me, by implication at least, with want of affection for my wife."

"No, Percy," returned the lady quickly. "I did not mean to say that. I only spoke of your manner towards her, which lacks the warmth a woman's heart requires. I have not said that you did not love her."

"I do not see how I can act differently; for I see no defect in my conduct," said the young man, with a repellant manner. "If my wife misinterprets the manner in which I treat her, and makes herself unhappy about it, that is no fault of mine. She ought to have the good sense to take me as I am, and not make herself wretched because I am not what I cannot be."

"You still misunderstand me, Percy," urged (sic) the the mother of Kate. "I did not say that your wife made herself wretched because your manner towards her was not different. I only suggested a modification of it, at least for the present, as a means of aiding in her return to a healthier state of mind. But we will say no more about this. I have frankly opened my mind to you, and thus far discharged my duty. You must now act as your own heart directs."

Percy showed no inclination to continue the subject. His manner plainly enough indicated that the conversation had given him no pleasure; and that he believed the mother of Kate to have exceeded the privilege of her position. When they parted, it was with the most formal politeness on both sides.

After Mrs. Harrison parted with Percy Edwards, the young man remained alone for nearly an hour. Sometimes he walked the floor with hurried steps, his manner greatly excited; sometimes he sat beside a table, with his head leaning upon his hand, so buried in thought as to be almost motionless; and sometimes he muttered to himself, as he aroused up from these fits of abstraction.

"Ah me!" he sighed, at last, rising slowly from his chair, and beginning to walk about, but with less agitation of manner than before exhibited. "This was a great mistake,—the one great error of my life. How blind I was not to have foreseen just such a result as this! I never had the smallest impulse of affection for her, and never can have. Both are unhappy in our bonds, and both will be so until death severs the unnatural tie. Ah me! A hundred thousand as a marriage portion, doubled on my own side, with half a million in prospect, does not put a single drop of honey in this cup, which grows more bitter with every draught. The worldly advantage is all very well. I am satisfied with that. But it comes at too heavy a cost. And poor Kate"—there was something of pity in the tone with which this was uttered—pity, not tenderness—"she has been the most wronged in this business. But the alliance was of her father's own seeking. His were the offered inducements, and I am not to be blamed if the temptation proved too strong for me. To a great extent, I can protect myself, though not fully. There are, thorns in my pillow which can neither be covered nor removed. Ah me! I wish Kate would seek, as I do, in coldness and indifference, the protection she needs. Her mother's observation is correct. There is no tenderness in my manner, and I have not meant that there should be. I have not treated her unkindly, for I wished to avoid all cause for complaint or reproach. I wished to stand clear before the world; and I am clear. If she beat herself against the bars of her cage, am I to blame? No, no! Let her yield to the necessity of her position, as I do. Let her avail herself of all the sources of forgetfulness within her reach—and there are many—and live passionless, if not happy. But she will not. If some speedy change do not take place, she cannot live a year. The world is quick in its imputation of wrong; and a whisper from her friends may thrill a thousand hearts with a suspicion of foul play, if she go down to the grave in so short a period after our marriage. And there is yet another consideration,—my interest in her father's large estate. How will that be affected? Having sacrificed so much for this consideration, it must not be abandoned now."

Edwards continued to move about the room, in deep reflection, for a considerable time longer. Then he went slowly up to his wife's chamber. She was lying upon the bed, with her face buried in a pillow. She did not stir, although his footfall was distinct upon the floor. Edwards went to the bedside, and leaning over, said, with more affection in his voice than he had ever used since their marriage, taking her hand in his, with a gentle pressure, at the same time—

"Kate, it grieves me to see you so ill both in body and mind."

There was an instant quiver in every limb, before so motionless; but the sufferer neither arose nor made any reply.

"Unless something be done for your relief," continued Mr. Edwards, in the same tone, "you cannot live. You know how much we are all afflicted, and how anxious we all feel on account of your loss of health and spirits."

The hand of his wife was still in his, and he held it with the same gentle pressure, that was now as gently returned. The impulse of Mr. Edwards was to remove his hand the instant Kate showed this consciousness of a tenderer manifestation than he was accustomed to give; but he restrained himself, and still let his hand rest upon hers. He felt that she was listening to him, and that he had the ability to influence her as he would, if he used the power of a well-counterfeited regard. After a few moments' silence, he went on:—

"I am sure that a change of air and a change of scene will do you good. This Doctor R—has already said, and you know that we all agree in the opinion. Now, will you not, to relieve the minds of your friends, even if you feel reluctant to quit this seclusion into which you have shrunk, make an effort? I am ready to go with you, at any moment. Come! arouse yourself; if not for your own sake, for ours, for mine."

The way in which this was said, more than the words themselves, acted like a charm upon Mrs. Edwards. The almost pulseless lethargy into which she had fallen passed off quickly, and rising up, she pushed back the matted hair from her face, and said, "I know you all think me perverse and unreasonable, and I may be so to some extent; but I will try to do as you wish. I feel as weak in mind and body as a child; and, like a child, I will submit myself to your direction. Only, Percy,"—her voice had a most touching pathos as she said this,—"*love me as a child!* Speak to me as gently, as tenderly as you did just now, and I will be the happiest being alive."

As she spoke, she leaned over towards her husband, and, burying her face on his bosom, sobbed aloud.

Cold-hearted as was Percy Edwards, this exhibition moved him. It was unexpected, and, therefore, he was not prepared to meet it in the way he would otherwise have done. As Kate lay weeping upon his bosom, and almost clinging to him, he experienced a change of feeling towards her. Pity melted into tenderness, and, on the impulse of the moment, he drew his arm around her, and, bending down, touched his lips to her forehead.

A happier moment the trembling wife had not known for years.

"You will make a short visit to Newport?" said Mr. Edwards, as Kate's feelings grew calmer.

"Oh, yes," she whispered, "if you wish me to do so."

"Only on account of your health," he replied, "I know it will do you good."

"Oh, certainly I will go. Forgive me for having before hesitated a moment; it was a childish weakness. But I will try hereafter to act with more reason."

The pressure of a tenderly spoken word revealed to Percy Edwards a hidden treasure in the love of a woman, worthy, truly worthy of a full reciprocation. Her heart was open and panting before him. Alas! for the man, that he could not prize the untold wealth he had only to reach forth his hand and take. But the lover of himself and the world is ever blind to what are life's real blessings. Thus blind was Percy Edwards.

Deluded into the belief that a genuine affection had been awakened in the breast of her husband, Kate felt the motions of a new life within her.

Satisfied that if he again fell back into his old habit of treating his wife, she would at once relapse into her former state of depression, Mr. Edwards maintained a certain appearance of affection, much as the effort cost him. It was wonderful to see the effect upon Mrs. Edwards. Her countenance became cheerful, her voice lost its even, passionless tone, and she evinced an interest in much that was passing around her. Preparations were immediately commenced for a visit to Newport, and in a week from the time she was aroused from the lethargy into which she had fallen, she left for that fashionable resort, in company with her husband and several friends.

www.ingramcontent.com/pod-product-compliance
Lightning Source LLC
Chambersburg PA
CBHW080212040426

42333CB00043B/2551